THE

Cranford

COMPANION

THE

Cranford

COMPANION

SUE BIRTWISTLE

&

SUSIE CONKLIN

BLOOMSBURY
LONDON · BERLIN · NEW YORK

To all the cast and crew

Cranford

2007 & 2009

With our gratitude, admiration and love

'It is the final word'

❖❖ CONTENTS ❖❖

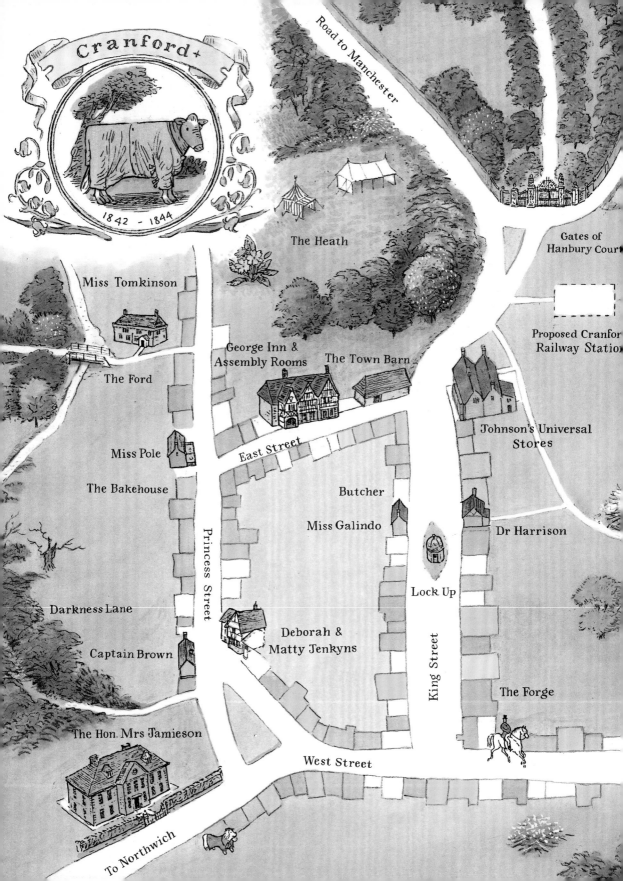

Cranford

1842 – 1844

Road to Manchester

The Heath

Gates of Hanbury Court

Proposed Cranford Railway Station

Miss Tomkinson

The Ford

George Inn & Assembly Rooms

The Town Barn

Johnson's Universal Stores

Miss Pole

East Street

The Bakehouse

Butcher

Miss Galindo

Dr Harrison

Princess Street

Lock Up

Darkness Lane

King Street

Captain Brown

Deborah & Matty Jenkyns

The Forge

The Hon. Mrs Jamieson

West Street

To Northwich

⊰◦⊱ The Beginnings ⊱◦⊰

TWENTY-FIVE SEASONS came and went between having the idea of making *Cranford* into a television drama and of seeing it on the screen. Of course, not all that time was taken up with *Cranford*, although it sometimes felt like it. We both worked on other projects, some of which jumped over many hurdles to get made, some of which fell in the final furlong when scripts had not only been commissioned but also written by well-known screenwriters. There is never a guarantee that your project will make it to the screen. And it seemed that might be the case with *Cranford*.

In 2000, Susie and I had been working on another dramatisation of an Elizabeth Gaskell novel, *Wives and Daughters*. At the end of filming, I was saying goodbye to Deborah Findlay and Barbara Flynn, who had played the spinster sisters, and Deborah said: 'You should read *Cranford*. We are all in there you know; it's all the same people.' It was to be a year – and another project later – before I took her advice. And it felt like coming home. I knew these women who set the tone for Cranford. I had grown up in a neighbourhood in Cheshire with many such women: wives, widows and spinsters who, while publicly giving men their place, were the backbone of that little society, and certainly gave it its tone. Next door but one lived the perfect replica of Miss Pole who, whilst ostensibly coming to fold sheets, would pass on all the gossip of the town in a whisper as the sheets were shaken out. Resourceful women, who stretched a little to go a long way but made everyone feel that they were fortunate to live there. And so we were.

I loved the everyday detail in the novel of the small lives of these women, and the book was very funny. So I was keen to see it dramatised, but didn't feel the material was robust enough to support the weight of a big television drama, which is what I wanted to make. But Deborah was right: the two main characters in *Cranford*, Miss Matty and Miss Deborah, were similar to the two spinster sisters in *Wives and Daughters*, only this time they were the centre of the drama. It was clear that they were the aunts who had brought up Elizabeth Gaskell when her mother had died during her infancy. Her father had sent her to live with them in Knutsford,

Miss Deborah and Miss Matty Jenkyns watch at their gate for the arrival of Mary Smith, the character who represents the young Elizabeth Gaskell in Cranford.

Cheshire, when she was only one, keeping her brother with him in London. She remembered it as a happy and secure childhood, and in her writings she would recount the goings-on in this town in many guises.

This was, maybe, the answer: to try to find these same characters in her other works and see if the material could be woven together to create one whole extensive narrative. It was a thrilling idea and it was at this point that I rang Susie. We had first worked together on *Pride and Prejudice* and I had been fortunate in that she had worked with me as Script Editor on every project I had produced since then. But this was a different proposition for us both. Should we take on this venture as writing partners, working together to interweave several of Gaskell's works to create the storylines for what we hoped would become an original drama? We were equally excited by this notion and agreed that it was insignificant that one of us lived in Colorado and the other in London.

So in early autumn 2001, I went to see Jane Tranter, Controller of BBC Drama. She was very trusting because there was not a word written on paper. I explained that we felt this would be a six-part drama about the small lives of ordinary people in a rural Cheshire market town in the

'This was a different house last year.' Matty reflects on a happier Christmas when she was at the heart of a house full of bustle and joy.

early 1840s. There would be no one narrative driving the action forward every week. Telling the story of these people through the accumulation of the domestic detail would be something that had not been seen on screen before, and the pace would naturally reflect that. Jane would need to feel very confident to commit to this, because scenes would unfold at the sort of measured rate that had become quite unfamiliar in contemporary drama.

Judi Dench.

And then I listed the elements that Susie and I considered the advantages of this project (well aware that a broadcaster or its finance department would find them less desirable): the main characters, the Amazons, were a group of ladies all over the age of sixty; the cast of leading actors would be enormous; we would need the best leading character actors in the country; we would try to show the workings of an entire town on screen; there would be many stories, multi-threaded so that everyone would be appearing in everyone else's stories, which meant long contracts for everyone; the action would take place over a whole year, requiring us to show all four seasons on screen; most locations would only be found outside London; the drama would need six hours of screen time; the leading actress, playing Miss Matty, would have to commit to seventeen weeks' continuous work; oh, and the ideal casting for this part would be Judi Dench, the most sought-after and busiest actress in the country.

Decisive as ever, Jane immediately commissioned us to write the Storylining Bible. This comprehensive document would summarise the project and its themes, charting all of the characters, their stories and the ways they interlinked, and laying out beat by beat the path each episode might follow. This would be sent out to potential co-producers to try to attract finance.

Gaskell wrote several novels, and many short stories and essays, not all of these easily accessible at that time. We were both working on other projects so we needed help and called in our friend, Pat Silburn, who managed to find copies of all her writing, read everything and draw up a short list of likely works to consider.

We eventually decided on the novels *Mr Harrison's Confessions* and *My Lady Ludlow*, and the essay *The Last Generation of England*. The former novel, a light comedy, gave us our younger romantic strand and using parts of *My Lady Ludlow* enabled us to portray a wider social picture by featuring the reigning aristocrat, her land agent and the young son of a gypsy. The essay, in which Gaskell sets down her memories of living in Knutsford, was a rich mine of material. Though hard to believe, the stories that we lifted from there – the cow in pyjamas, the cat swallowing the lace, the tea tray concealed under the sofa – were true. When interwoven with *Cranford*, these would give us a picture of the whole society.

We set about filleting the books, deciding which characters and incidents we would use. We ended up with more than forty characters to be threaded into each other's complex stories, without the joins being visible. Early in 2002, we met in New York and devised an index-card system, different colours for different characters, plot-lines and incidents. There were hundreds of cards, which we placed on the floor that we had divided into 'episodes'. We moved amongst them: 'Too much green story in Episode Two; let's move some to Episode Three.' It was a very literal way of seeing how all the stories were interweaving and whether the progression for each character was logical. This was all put on to computer to be refined and, in May, we delivered the Storylining Bible on which Jane authorised funding for the scripts to be written. We were both thrilled when Heidi Thomas joined us in July as the scriptwriter. All our script meetings were held in my house and Heidi vividly remembers the many walks from the tube station across Brook Green: 'Magnolia trees in blossom in spring, parched grass in summer, kicking through leaves in autumn, and once stumbling in snow.' What she hadn't anticipated was that this journey would be repeated over many years as the project stumbled too.

It wouldn't be overstating to say that the scripting process for *Cranford* was the most complex that either Heidi or we had ever experienced. Together we worked in detail through every beat of all the stories. It was a wonderfully creative time of speculation where we licensed each other to suggest the wildest, most improbable ideas on the premise that ideas spark other ideas, which might finally lead to a great one. Characters from the different books had already been merged, but here we fused them further; and other characters, like Harry Gregson, found a fuller life mapped out by Heidi. The final draft scripts were delivered and received with joy by Jane in December 2003. Even though we now had our dream casting of Judi Dench attached as Miss Matty, it took a whole year to secure the

finance, which we had in place for just two happy days in December 2004 before the BBC made 15 per cent cuts to all budgets and, as a consequence, we lost our co-production money. The project was shelved.

Sue, Susie and Heidi after the read-through, April 2007.

Despite the fact that in March 2005 we were firmly advised by the BBC to put *Cranford* 'out of mind for ever', throughout that year and the next we continued to chase possible finance and tried various ways to make it more affordable. We struggled to squeeze the stories into four and a half hours, with Heidi writing a new ninety-minute first episode, then we reconfigured it as a five-part drama. Finally, in 2006 – December again – we secured US co-finance from WGBH in Boston and BBC Worldwide, with BBC Drama Productions being the main financier. At last, in January 2007, we were given the green light and went into pre-production.

We started filming on a beautiful April day in bluebell woods. We finished shooting in August – on the most perfect English evening one could picture. It is almost impossible to imagine that, in between, we had worked in more or less continuous rain. Post-production continued, even as the first episode was being screened in November. That episode was

watched by ten million people and the BBC, which had been going through particularly difficult times, both politically and publicly, celebrated its success, some executives even crediting it with salvaging the BBC's reputation in the eyes of the nation.

We wanted to write this book because there was so much more material in the novels than we could use – wonderful detail which informed the scripts, but which we were not always able to bring directly into play. We also wanted to celebrate the work of the several hundreds of cast and crew who made *Cranford* what it is. So it's a mongrel book: the first part explores the world of Cranford; the latter part takes you in amongst the cast and crew, both at work and off set.

Elizabeth Gaskell.

'In the Spring a young man's fancy lightly turns to thoughts of love.' Jem Hearne courts the Jenkyns' serving maid, Martha.

In many ways the little society that we formed to make *Cranford* echoed the spirit of the town we were putting on screen. The same goodwill, mutual support, pleasure in working together and sense of community flourished in our company, where the whole became much more than the sum of the parts, a little of which we hope will be apparent by the end of this book.

A word of warning: everything in this book references <u>our</u> *Cranford*, the world of Cranford that we created for the television screen. Of course, that is principally Gaskell's *Cranford* too, but we took many liberties with her material so there are variations from the novel, but this became our reality – and is the reality of this book. We felt partly licensed to make changes after reading Gaskell's letters: she'd been commissioned by Dickens to write a story for his magazine *Household Words*. When the story was successful, he commissioned a second, then a third… If she had known it was to end up a novel, she said, she would not have killed off Captain Brown in Chapter Two. We took this as permission to keep him alive; one small alteration of the many that we ventured.

Cheerful in spite of the weather: the production needed an unprecedented number of umbrellas as work continued in unremitting rain for much of the shoot.

The changes – and any mistakes – are entirely ours. The genius is Elizabeth Gaskell's.

Sue Birtwistle & Susie Conklin, June 2010

❧ The Wide World ☙
by Jenny Uglow

AT THE START OF the 1840s, Miss Matilda Jenkyns and her friends are standing outside Johnson's shop in Cranford. They gaze at the announcements of new Paris fashions. They wonder whether green tea is preferable to China tea, which sounds so exotic. Most exciting of all, they gasp over the announcement that the conjuror Signor Brunoni intends to give a performance in the Assembly Rooms – would it be proper, Miss Matty wonders, to wear a turban, perhaps in sea green, her favourite colour?

While the ladies are principally concerned as to how such small things will go down in Cranford, they are also dreaming – looking far away across the oceans, across the world. The small Cheshire town they live in is not entirely a backwater. Its inhabitants read the papers and hear news from the nearby manufacturing town of Manchester, and from relatives in Edinburgh or London. The events in the wider world, and in their own

Miss Matty, Mrs Forrester, Miss Tomkinson and Miss Pole discuss the poster advertising the forthcoming Magic Show to be given by the exotic Signor Brunoni.

troubled nation, make a subtle impact on all their lives. They also have their own stories and visions of distant lands, and their imaginations stretch around the globe.

Peter Jenkyns, for example, the errant brother of Deborah and Matty Jenkyns, ran off to sea as a boy and vanished to India. Many people thought he had disappeared for ever. But Miss Matty is sure he is still alive – there are rumours that he has even become 'Aga Jenkyns of Chunderayabad' – so the young Mary Smith decides to try and reach him, simply by posting a letter. Britain rules the waves: ships can stop at a series of colonial ports on the West Coast of Africa before reaching the Cape of Good Hope and then setting sail for India. Such voyages take weeks, but things are about to speed up and the great globe will grow smaller with the steamships just coming into service. In 1840 a P&O mail service, using a steam paddle-ship, begins

running from Falmouth to Alexandria, with another Cunard service crossing from Liverpool to Boston. Only fifteen miles or so from quiet Cranford, Liverpool – teeming with traders, its warehouses packed with exotic goods – is becoming a vast port, the gateway to the New World, where thousands of desperate Irish and English emigrants will embark, hoping to find new lives. In July 1843, Isambard Kingdom Brunel's *Great Britain* is launched, the first screw-propelled iron liner, setting out two years later to cross the Atlantic.

The British flag is flying in the furthest corners of the world. In New Zealand, Maori chiefs surrender sovereignty to Queen Victoria in the treaty of Waitangi of 1840; in Australia, Edward John Eyre, with his Aborigine companion Wylie, crosses the Nullarbor Plain, from Adelaide to the west coast; and in Antarctica, in a great expedition between 1839 and 1843, James Clark Ross discovers and claims 'Victoria Land'. British trading posts are dotted throughout Malaya, and from the late eighteenth century British ships have been carrying cargoes of opium from India to China, bringing back tea in return. In 1839 the Opium War begins after

The launch of Isambard Kingdom Brunel's steamship Great Britain.

The Manchester to Liverpool railway in 1833.

the Canton authorities, alarmed by the rise in addiction, try to stop this trade. When the war ends three years later China gives rights in five ports to British traders, also ceding the island of Hong Kong.

At home, the whole nation is changing. A network of railways is spreading, built by the bands of navvies who seem so threatening to the Cranford townsfolk. Across the country, by the middle of the nineteenth century there are 250,000 navvies (whose name came from 'navigator'), many of them poor labourers from Ireland working in organised gangs, living in shanty towns put up by the line they are building. Paid well, they drink as hard as they work, often going on a binge for days, and many people fear their arrival in the neighbourhood.

But the railways also bring fun. In 1841 Thomas Cook introduces the first railway excursions, taking a temperance outing from Leicester to Loughborough. A year later, on 13 June 1842, Queen Victoria takes her first train journey. Newspapers and mail reach Cheshire faster by train than in the old coaching days. People hear fine accounts of London – a city that few of Miss Matty's friends have ever visited. The streets of the capital are paved and lit with brilliant gas lighting, the shops have great plate-glass windows, and Barry has begun rebuilding the Houses of Parliament – a task that will take twenty years.

In the cities, an educated middle class is emerging, and a swathe of new institutions are founded to cater to its cultural needs. In 1839 the first Henley Regatta takes place, and much nearer home, the first Grand National at Aintree. A year later, the Royal Botanic Gardens at Kew open to the public, and the year after that Charles Dickens – Captain Brown's favourite author, shunned by the old-fashioned Deborah Jenkyns – publishes a new novel, *The Old Curiosity Shop*. For poetry-lovers Tennyson publishes his *Collected Poems*, including 'Locksley Hall', so admired by Miss Matty and Mr Holbrook, and in 1843 Elizabeth Gaskell's hero, William Wordsworth, becomes Poet Laureate.

Queen Victoria in 1843.

The choicest gossip, however, concerns the kingdom's young queen, Victoria, crowned in 1838. Not all the news is rosy as Victoria is determined, and can be wilful. In May 1839, when her much-loved advisor Lord Melbourne resigns as prime minister, his opposite number Robert Peel cannot form a government because Victoria refuses to abide by convention and change her Whig ladies of the bedchamber for Tories. Her behaviour towards her lady-in-waiting, Lady Flora Hastings, whom she tries to banish from court on suspicion that she is pregnant – in fact she is dying of liver cancer – outrages London society, and she is hissed on her way to Ascot in her carriage. But the little queen's popularity soars again when she marries her cousin, Albert of Saxe-Coburg, in February 1840. She is as romantic as any young Cranford girl, dreaming of her lover: 'Such a pretty mouth with delicate moustaches,' she swoons, 'and a beautiful figure, broad shoulders and fine waist; my heart is quite going…' When their first son is born on 9 November 1841 (the future king Edward VII), the whole nation rejoices.

This is the kind of news that Cranford relishes, although there are more serious things to trouble people outside their sheltered world. The rapid industrialisation of the last fifty years has altered the face of the country and towns like Bradford and Glasgow have grown eight fold between 1801 and 1851, as people stream in from the country to work in factories and mills. Slums are springing up like mushrooms. Typhus and cholera are rife, and poor families are often packed into cellars. In 1840, a visitor from the Domestic Home Mission in Manchester describes seeing a woman who has just given birth to a child, lying on a few bits of dirty sacking on bare flags, with another near-naked child nearby: 'The husband said that he had neither candle, food, nor money.'

There is growing anxiety about the terrible working conditions and very slowly, as statistics are gathered and campaigners lobby Parliament, a series of reforms are put in place – notably, the beginning of a drive for education, of the kind that horrifies conservatives like Cranford's Lady Ludlow. Charity schools and Sunday schools proliferate and the first bill is introduced into Parliament, by Lord Brougham, for public education.

Ripples of widespread distress and unrest reach Cranford ears. After an outcry over the rising price of bread, the Anti-Corn-Law League, based in Manchester, fights for a repeal of protectionist laws banning the import of cheap foreign grain that have kept the price of corn and bread absurdly high. Many workers, however, are suspicious of this largely middle-class movement, thinking that cheaper bread will mean that masters can lower their wages. Instead they unite to publish a People's Charter, demanding universal manhood suffrage, the removal of property qualifications for voters, annual parliaments and a secret ballot. The first Chartist National Convention is held in February 1839 in London, and that summer their first petition is presented to Parliament, only to be swiftly rejected. There are riots in Birmingham and further disturbances around the country. In a Chartist rising in Newport, South Wales, twenty-four people are killed and in this area the ill feeling slowly swells into the 'Rebecca Riots' of 1842.

The misery is intensified by four years of bad harvests, which leave the poor on the verge of starvation, and by a series of bank crashes and recessions in trade, when factories and mills shut down, throwing workers on the street. This is the start of the 'Hungry Forties'. In August 1842, Chartists and some Anti-Corn-Law followers campaign together for a general strike in Lancashire and the Midlands. Two thousand troops are sent to Manchester in anticipation of an expected Chartist riot, led by General Napier. 'This is the chimney of the world,' writes Napier. 'Rich rascals, poor rogues, drunken ragamuffins and prostitutes… What a place! The entrance to hell realised!'

The situation provokes some powerful responses. In *Past and Present*, published in 1843, Thomas Carlyle looks back on a vanished world and

fulminates against the new machine-driven, materialist, soulless age.
Manchester, 'Cottonopolis', seems the embodiment of this heartless
striving. Men and women operate the new steam looms for hours at
a stretch, and children run below, picking up the fluff – all inhaling dust
and fluff that ruins their lungs and costs many lives. In the country they
had been poor, but at least they could breathe. As the wife of William
Gaskell, the hard-working junior minister at Cross Street Unitarian
Chapel, Elizabeth Gaskell comes face to face with Manchester's suffering
poor, and in the early 1840s the couple throw themselves into relief work,
distributing food, soup tickets and clothing.

By 1842 Gaskell is thirty-two, with three young daughters. As often as
she can, she escapes to the small Cheshire town of Knutsford, where she
had grown up with her Aunt Lumb and her aunt's circle of independent-
minded women. This haven, with all its eccentricities, is the opposite of
the threatening, smoky city. Change is bound to arrive, as she and her
characters know, but she feels that it is vital to carry the little town's
values of friendship, kindness and mutual support into the wider world.

*Women at work
in a lace factory.
People abandoned
rural areas in great
numbers to find
employment in the
mills of large towns.*

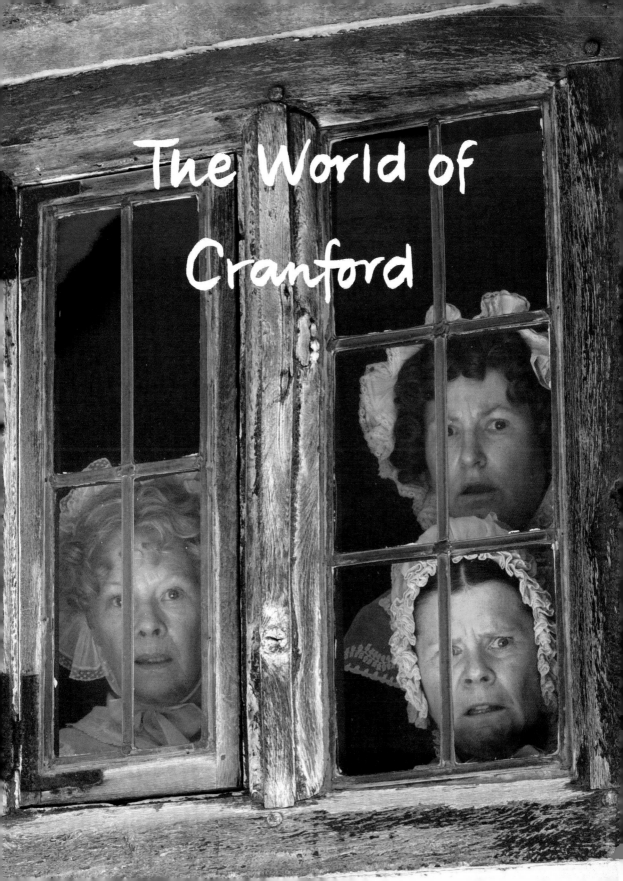

⊰ Our Society ⊱

NESTLING in good farming land on the mid-Cheshire plains, Cranford is 'a world entire unto itself'. This small market town of two thousand souls is barely fifteen miles from Manchester, but no Industrial Revolution has come near enough to trouble it. Silk and cotton are still occasionally woven on hand looms in lofts above the cottages and the town makes shift with one carpenter and a part-time constable. It is, however, on the main coaching route from both Liverpool and Chester to London, and the Royal Mail coaches twice daily interrupt the tranquillity of the town to deliver and pick up post and passengers.

No single architectural style holds sway in Cranford. Black and white timbered buildings, so typical of this part of Cheshire, rub shoulders with tiny red brick houses and pink-washed cottages. Some roofs are thatched, some are tiled. The unmade streets curve and meander, sometimes too narrow for two pig carts to pass each other, sometimes widening enough for coaches to turn round and for people to linger there and chat. It is 'a very picturesque place. The houses are anything but regular, they may be mean in their details but altogether they look well; they have not that unrelieved front which many towns of pretension present. Here and there a bow window, every now and then a gable, occasionally a projecting upper storey throws light or shadow on the street.'

The district in which Cranford is set is inhabited by several landed proprietors from very distinguished families, which take the lead in a rigid social hierarchy. When the oldest son inherits, unmarried daughters or younger brothers' widows from these old families often retire to live on a small annuity in or near the town. Although poorer than the professional men and their wives, they are always treated with deference by them. A social grade lower come the single or widowed ladies who, though not well-off, are probably more financially secure than the aristocratic ladies. Then come the shopkeepers, who have more money and so can dare to be original in when they dine and what they eat. Lower down come the poor, both respectable (and therefore worthy of charity) and unrespectable (therefore unworthy of any attention but gossip). Clinging on to the outskirts of society is a set of young men 'ready for

The weekly market in King Street: farmers arrive early with their animals to sell or barter.

mischief and brutality, and every now and then dropping off the pit's brink into crime'. If they are apprehended, the town has a Lock-up where they can be kept secure whilst waiting to be brought before the magistrate, Sir Charles Maulver.

Commerce

The significant streets of the town can be counted on the fingers of one hand. The two main thoroughfares – King Street and Princess Street – would run parallel to each other, if only they were straight. Together with East Street and West Street, they form the town into a rough square shape. King Street, as its name suggests, is the prime street and it is surprisingly wide for such a small place. Happily so, for it must accommodate the weekly market, the rights for which were granted by Royal Charter in 1292. Farmers from the surrounding countryside arrive early, bringing animals

(both live and dead) to sell or barter. The produce, displayed on carts or spread simply on hessian cloth, always reflects the seasons.

Market days are usually noisy, with the blacksmith's forge and anvil being in demand, but in spring when newborn animals – lambs, piglets, chicks and goslings – are being sold, the farmers have to shout even louder over their cries to attract customers. Most householders in Cranford keep some animals in their garden: chickens, perhaps, for the daily eggs; a goose to fatten for Michaelmas; a pig to kill at Christmas. Cheshire, renowned for its cheese and butter, has rich farming soil with a healthy rainfall and there is always a colourful display of fruits and vegetables for those who can afford them. In autumn, plums, apples, pears and quince sit alongside chestnuts knocked from the trees by young boys hoping to earn some money. Rabbits and wood pigeons to be skinned or plucked hang next to sheep fleeces, tanned cow hides, and onions strung together to store through the cold months. In winter, cabbages, carrots, potatoes and

Miss Pole seizes Harry Gregson when she catches him selling fish that he has poached, and reports him to Lady Ludlow's land agent Mr Carter.

turnips are piled high. Blocks of salt from Mr Buxton's salt mines in Northwich are sold by weight, being vital for the preserving of meats and fish through the winter. It is likely that some of the fish on sale will have been poached from the local rivers by the likes of Harry, the son of the notorious ne'er-do-well Job Gregson. Women from the town sell homemade goods: humbugs, cordials, preserves, silk buttons and knitted garments (socks, gloves, scarves and pullovers being popular with those who cannot knit their own or have no wife to do so).

The main shops of the town are also to be found on King Street. Miss Galindo's millinery shop is three doors down from the shoe shop. The town's two cobblers both make and mend shoes, but business is not so brisk that they can afford to give up their second job as the carriers of the town's sedan chair. They are most frequently called out by the Hon. Mrs Jamieson who refuses to walk even short distances. Then they must remove their leather aprons and don long frock coats and ancient powdered wigs that make them look as if they have stepped from one of Mr Hogarth's pictures.

Mr Gidman, one of Cranford's most successful businessmen, has the shop next door, which sells baskets, brushes, toys and cane chairs. He is a cooper by trade, specialising in barrels and churns, and he has a large

Bonnets discreetly displayed in Miss Galindo's millinery shop window.

> Miss Matilda Jenkyns
>
> Mr Josiah Johnson hosts a presentation of This Season's Silks & Fashions.
>
> Tea will be served to favoured clients, on Thursday 27th April, at two o'clock in the afternoon.

A prized invitation: Mr Johnson invites his favourite clients to a preview of the new fashions.

workshop on the riverbank beyond the Ford, where many of Cranford's men, women and children are employed to strip the willow. His daughter, Margaret, was once interviewed for a position as a maid at Hanbury Court but, because her father had taught her to read and help cast up his accounts, Lady Ludlow refused to take her and she is now parlour maid to Mr Buxton at The Glebe. Lady Ludlow, the Liege Lady of Cranford, has very strong views about educating the working classes. She believes it would lead to the breakdown of law and order and result in civic strife. She has founded her own Charity School for young girls where they are taught to knit, to sew, to iron and to say their prayers: all that is needed to become a good servant. The ladies of Cranford are encouraged to visit the school to help teach these skills and are rewarded each summer with an invitation to Lady Ludlow's garden party at Hanbury Court, the social event of their year.

Although Hanbury Court itself is two miles distant from the marketplace, the gates to Hanbury stand imposingly just a short walk down King Street from Johnson's Universal Stores, the largest shop in Cranford. Being merely 'in trade', Mr and Mrs Johnson would not in the normal run of things be invited to the Hanbury Garden Party, but because Mr Johnson has been made Mayor of Cranford, this event is part of their social calendar too. Their business has grown from a modest shop to an impressive modern store, which is now the social hub of the town. Their boast is that they can provide anything required and can order from Manchester, or from London even!

The Amazons

The town is dominated by the Amazons, the older ladies who set the tone and keep careful watch to check that all is done as it should be. Certainly men live in Cranford but, having arrived, they always seem to disappear. Some are accounted for by being with their regiment or away all week on business in Manchester. The ones who remain are generally too terrified of being the only man at an evening party with the ladies of Cranford. The doctor and the attorney both prefer their slippers and a hot supper at home. The ladies at their card parties often rejoice that there is no gentleman to be attended to, or to find conversation for, and they congratulate themselves on the snugness and gentility of the evening.

The ladies of Cranford find themselves sufficient for all else that needs to be attended to: for keeping their gardens trim and free of weeds and chasing away young boys – or geese – who might have designs on their choice flowers; for keeping their maidservants in order; for having firm opinions about questions of politics and literature without troubling to have any knowledge of these subjects; for knowing everyone's business in the parish; and for tender concern for each other when a friend is in distress. A man is not needed for these offices. As is often remarked: 'A man is *so* in the way in the house.'

Miss Pole and Mrs Forrester are usually the first to check the new ribbons in Johnson's, but rarely make a purchase.

All the ladies have their individual eccentricities and opinions, which are well known amongst them, though frequently ignored. Occasionally a little quarrel will erupt and be played out in 'a few peppery words and angry jerks of the head', but for the most part goodwill exists between them. They are full of kindness to 'The Poor' of the parish, in a somewhat dictatorial way. They cook and sew for them, give them remedies for illnesses and advice on child care, though none herself has had a child. They do everything but educate them.

The ladies always wear the same well-preserved clothes in a style that is 'quite independent of fashion'. When in Cranford, they justify this by saying to each other: 'What does it signify how we dress here at Cranford where everyone knows us?' When away from home, they use the same reasoning: 'What does it signify how we dress here, where nobody knows us?'

Social Etiquette

Miss Deborah Jenkyns is the arbiter of social etiquette in Cranford. If anyone is in doubt of the right thing to do in any particular situation, they might think: 'What would Miss Jenkyns do?' There is a strict code for visiting which is passed on to all newcomers. Calling hours are between twelve noon and three o'clock in the afternoon and one should never linger longer than a quarter of an hour. Of course, it would be most impolite to keep looking at the clock, so a newcomer is advised never to engage in interesting topics, in case the time is forgotten in the pleasure of the conversation.

A series of small parties are given on the arrival of a visitor to any friend's house. These are taken very seriously, with all sitting rather gravely in their best dresses. The ladies arrive soon after four o'clock and might take a half-hour in the dining parlour to unburden themselves of their outer garments and overshoes, and to unpin the hems of their dresses (lifted to protect them against the mud) before being shown into the drawing room. Card tables will have been set up by the hostess with new packs of cards, for which it is customary for guests to pay by discreetly placing a shilling under the candlestick. The game of choice in Cranford is Preference and little conversation is allowed to interrupt the concentration of the players. Cards are a serious business!

Tea trays are later brought in by the serving maid and placed in the centre of each table. It is a fact that most of the ladies have little money and have difficulty making ends meet, but poverty is never mentioned. Financial struggles are concealed under a smiling face and it is generally

At Lady Ludlow's annual garden party, Miss Deborah and Miss Matty are shocked to hear the news that the railway is coming to Cranford.

agreed that it is 'vulgar' to be ostentatious in the provision of eatables or drinkables. The china will be fine, but the bread and butter will be wafer-thin. 'Elegant Economy' is always the order of the day and there exists a wonderful *esprit de corps* amongst the Amazons to support each other in these attempts to conceal deficiencies in hospitality.

One consequence of this unacknowledged lack of means (and some would say it is a happy one) is that Cranford keeps early hours. At half past eight, it will be announced that the servants have arrived with lanterns to accompany their various mistresses safely home. The card games will be concluded and accounts settled. The ladies will struggle back into their outer garments and by nine o'clock the party will have concluded. By ten o'clock, the whole town will be abed.

May Day

When the hedgerows are at their gayest, displaying cow parsley and May blossom, and the bluebells are at their best, the whole town – high and low – gathers on the Heath to celebrate May Day. So renowned is Cranford's celebration that people set off early from outlying districts to bear witness to it. Although sanctioned by the presence of the Rector and the Liege Lady, this is an ancient Pagan celebration of fertility and many of its rituals are unchanged since medieval times.

The people of the town wake early in anticipation of the day and mistresses find their serving maids already on their knees sanding the front steps. This is a tradition particular to Cranford, where coloured sands are funnelled through cones made of paper into elaborate patterns of swirls and spirals, such as might decorate a Paisley shawl or the floors of a Moorish mosque.

No other work will be done in Cranford today for this, like Mothering Sunday, is a universal holiday. The townsfolk will have laid out their best clothes overnight and many days' planning will have gone into their trimming. Johnson's Stores has done brisk business the previous week as half-yards of ribbon have been considered at length and purchased. Old lace, inherited from grandmothers, has been washed and pinned flat to dry. Brooches, required to cover defects on dresses, have been worried over. In the poorer houses, the little boys black their faces and prepare to run wild all day.

*May Day:
The girls from Lady Ludlow's Charity School dance round the Maypole.*

Mr Johnson, the newly appointed Mayor, and his wife watch the festivities.

In the company of Dr Morgan and Dr Harrison, Mrs Rose, Mrs Forrester, Miss Tomkinson and Caroline enjoy the dancing.

In the barn, across the street from the bunting-decked Johnson's Stores, the town band tunes up with a verse of 'Now is the Month of Maying' and a pint of ale from the George Inn. There will be many more of both before the day is done. This is the one day of the year when misrule might be overlooked by the ladies of Cranford. The single young working men of the district are already picking cowslips to decorate their hats and discussing their chances of becoming better acquainted with some of the pretty serving maids, who are normally so strictly guarded by their mistresses.

On the Heath, the Maypole has been erected and the ribbons secured. A wooden stage has been constructed and decorated with ivy and wild flowers from the wood. Guy ropes are tightened on the tea tent and the ale tent. Many sideshows are being set up: Punch and Judy, try-your-luck games, gypsy fortune-tellers, skittles, archery. Hard-earned wages will disappear in these tents and stalls today.

Each year, one of the town lads is picked to be 'Jack-in-the-Green', the body of a man inside a bush, which is said to represent the rebirth of nature after winter. A reassuring idea but a rather wild manifestation of it, as the young man is licensed to cavort all day long, regularly refreshed with ale. Strapped into the costume – constructed from wickerwork, bent into the shape of a giant bush and covered entirely with greenery – he will lead the procession as it sets off from the barn, dancing through the streets all the way to the Heath.

It is Jack-in-the-Green's job to clear the path for those that follow and he will dash at the young boys who are dared to stop the way and send them squealing to safety. The town band comes next with the dancing morris men, dressed all in white except for the cross-gartered ribbons and bells on their legs. They jog-trot along, waving white handkerchiefs in the air. Carried in the sedan chair is the young girl who has been chosen to be the May Queen, followed by her attendants and the boy who bears the crown.

Many farm carts have been cleaned and pressed into service to carry the various pageants organised by the tradesmen. The Mayor and Mrs Johnson ride on the most splendid one, cleverly advertising their new lines. The Charity School girls dressed in their Sunday best ride on another, watched over anxiously by their matron. For several days they have been

Notorious poacher Job Gregson earns honest money on May Day by playing his pipe with the town band.

excused from their worsted-work lessons, to practise the complicated dance patterns required to weave and unweave the ribbons round the Maypole. This afternoon, they are to be watched by their patroness!

Lady Ludlow, accompanied by her land agent Mr Carter and her friend Miss Galindo, always arrives last. She will stay just long enough to crown the May Queen with a few gracious words and applaud the girls from her Charity School when they dance. She will walk amongst the townsfolk, acknowledging those who are invited to her garden party. She will spend money at the more respectable sideshows and, her duties at an end, she will be driven back to Hanbury Court, where she will dine alone.

Meanwhile, on the Heath, the band will play late into the evening and the behaviour of the young men will grow more raucous. The Amazons will gather to walk home together, casting anxious glances backwards to see if they can determine where their holidaying maidservants are in the gathering dusk. Miss Matty will remark: 'The stars are so beautiful!' and then remember that the earth is moving constantly and regret she brought it to mind, for it's a notion that always makes her feel so insecure and dizzy.

Lady Ludlow fulfils one of her many duties as Liege Lady of the town by crowning Helen Hutton as the May Queen.

❖❖ The People of Cranford ❖❖

Miss Deborah Jenkyns

Miss Matty Jenkyns

Mr Peter Jenkyns

Jem Hearne

Martha

Tilly Hearne

Mary Smith

Clara Smith

Mr Holbrook

Mrs Forrester

Miss Pole

Bertha

Miss Tomkinson

Caroline Tomkinson

The Hon. Mrs Jamieson

Lady Glenmire

Captain Brown

Jessie Brown

Major Gordon

Mr Johnson

Mrs Johnson

Lady Ludlow   Septimus Hanbury   Sir Charles Maulver

Miss Galindo   Mr Carter   Harry Gregson

Bella Gregson   Job Gregson   Dr Marshland

Dr Harrison   Mrs Rose   Dr Morgan

Mr Buxton

William Buxton

Erminia Whyte

Mrs Bell

Peggy Bell

Edward Bell

Reverend Hutton

Sophy Hutton

Walter Hutton

Lizzie Hutton

Helen Hutton

Signor Brunoni

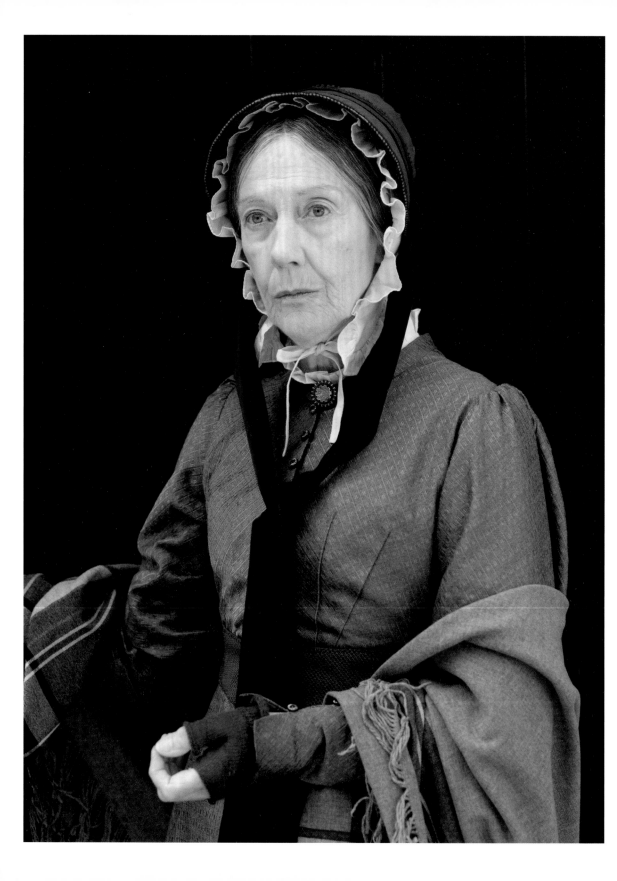

Miss Deborah &
Miss Matty Jenkyns

MISS DEBORAH and Miss Matty Jenkyns grew up in the Rectory with their younger brother, Peter, children of John Jenkyns, the Rector, and his wife, Molly. Deborah, the oldest, was the favourite of her father and helped him copy out his sermons, both admiring the literary style of Dr Johnson. Matty liked nothing more than to help her mother run the Rectory and especially enjoyed cutting flowers from the garden and placing them in all the rooms. Her mother called her 'my right hand'. Each morning, their father would make them write out on one side of a piece of paper what they hoped to achieve in the day, and in the evening, on the opposite side, what in fact had happened. Once, as they sat by Deborah's bedroom fire finishing this task, Deborah told Matty that she would like to marry an archdeacon and help write his sermons. Matty, who considered herself unambitious, thought she would be content to have a home to run and children to care for, as she had always been fond of little children, and they of her.

When Peter was born, he quickly became the darling of both Matty and his mother. His father's plan was for him to win great honours at school and carry them through to Cambridge and a fine career, but things did not work out as hoped. At Shrewsbury, the sole honour he won was 'the reputation of being the best fellow that ever was, and of being captain of the school in the art of practical joking'. His hoaxing became so serious that he was removed from school and, as the Rector could not afford a private tutor, he decided to coach the boy himself for his university examinations. But Peter was always too fond of mischief and this was to bring disaster on the family.

On a spring day, when Peter was sixteen and the lilac was in full bloom and Deborah had been a fortnight gone to stay with friends in Newcastle, Peter went into her room and dressed himself in the gown, shawl and bonnet that Deborah often used to wear in Cranford. He wanted to give the town 'something to talk about'. Without thinking of the shame it might bring to Deborah, he made a pillow into the shape

Miss Deborah had 'so long taken the lead in Cranford that they hardly knew how to give a party' without her advice.

of a baby, covered it in long white clothes, and walked up and down the Rectory garden, talking to 'the baby'. A crowd of twenty or more gathered and watched in amazement through the gates at what appeared to be Miss Deborah returned with a newborn baby. This is the sight that met the Rector when he came home. In his fury, he lifted up his walking cane and beat his son in front of the townsfolk. Peter stood white-faced and as still as a statue to be flogged until his father ran out of strength. Afterwards, Peter found his mother and Matty in the storeroom making cowslip wine. Without telling them of the beating, he asked for God's blessing on his mother, kissed her and then disappeared.

For days they thought Peter had killed himself and the ponds were dragged and the barns searched. Eventually he sent news that he was in Liverpool and had signed on to a warship to fight the French. His parents hastened to the docks, but they were too late; the ship had sailed. His mother was never to see him again. In her grief, she gradually lost her mind and died within the year. His father blamed himself and was a broken man, relying more and more on Deborah to help him fulfil his parish duties. She told Matty that even if she had a hundred offers, she never would marry and leave her father. Matty thought this was much to her credit, even if it was not likely that she had so many offers; in fact, probably not one.

Matty felt she could best help by quietly assuming all the duties of running the Rectory. But she'd had her own private sorrow to keep hidden for nearly a year from her grieving family. Just before Peter's disappearance, she had received a proposal of marriage from Mr Thomas Holbrook, second cousin to Miss Pole and an independent farmer of some consequence with a fine old house at Woodley. They had met at a dance in the Assembly Rooms and he had been an occasional visitor at the Rectory since. He had befriended the sixteen-year-old Peter and taught him to fish. Bit by bit, he and Matty fell in love and he asked her to be his wife. But Matty was aware that he would not be considered enough of a gentleman by her father or sister, who would have felt that she was marrying below her rank. He 'spoke the dialect of the country to perfection and constantly used it in conversation' and Matty's family was related to aristocracy. These things mattered very much to Miss Deborah.

But Matty, knowing his superior qualities and his true kindness to everyone, felt that if her family were given time to get to know him better

they would happily give their consent. She was encouraged in this thought by noticing Peter's fondness for Mr Holbrook, and she felt too that her mother had guessed that she wanted to marry him and had voiced no opposition. But it was then that Peter ran away and Matty knew that any other strain on the family at this time would break it entirely. So she met Mr Holbrook in the lane that leads from the Rectory to Woodley and told him that she could not marry him, but did not give him the reason. Mrs Forrester, passing by, noticed that Matty was crying and so agitated that she was pulling the petals off the primroses she was holding.

Since that time, Thomas Holbrook avoided going into Cranford and Matty shut up her love close in her heart and kept her sorrow to herself. Forty years later, she would say: 'I have known people with very good hearts, and very clever minds too, who were not what some people reckoned refined, but who were both true and tender.'

Elegant Economy

When the Rector died some time after, Deborah and Matty were obliged to leave the Rectory and, instead of keeping three maids and a man, they had to move to a small house in Cranford, and be content with a servant-of-all-work. They took some of the Rectory furniture – the two chairs they placed on either side of the hearth were the ones their parents had used – but most was too big for the smaller rooms. Instead of the large drawing room, they have to make shift with a cosy parlour, sometimes separated by a curtain from an equally diminutive dining parlour. Directly across the hall is the kitchen with its blacked cooking range, large sink with a water pump and a cool stone larder. Two dressers flank the other walls and a large scrubbed wooden table fills the middle. On this, bread is kneaded, vegetables are chopped and preserves are tied up by Martha, the servant.

Up the wooden staircase, there are three simple bedchambers. In their rooms, Deborah and Matty sleep in the beds they had as young women in the Rectory. Guests do not often come to stay and it is Mary Smith who most frequently uses the third, smaller bedroom when she visits. All of the bedrooms have a fireplace, but fires are only lit there if someone is ill. Martha sleeps in the attic, a large and very chilly room, which causes Matty some anxiety in the winter. But Martha, having grown up on a farm and being used to outdoor work in all weathers, claims not to notice.

Fires are always lit in the parlour in the evenings and Matty envies Deborah's skill in instructing Martha on the proper way to make a fire. Their father's books have pride of place on the shelves in the dining parlour and Matty still uses her mother's sewing basket. The clock on the parlour mantelpiece regulates the day, as it once did in the Rectory. The china is delicate eggshell; the old-fashioned silver glitters with polishing. Deborah says it is important to live genteelly, even if circumstances compel them to simplicity.

Matty admires her sister as 'quite the woman of business who always judges for herself'. She wears a cravat and has the appearance of a strong-minded woman, although she despises the modern idea of a woman being equal to a man. 'Equal, indeed!' – she knows they are superior in every way. But, although it is Deborah who assumes the masculine role – who decides where their money will be invested, what allowance will be made for clothes, and the terms of employment for their servant – it is Matty

Miss Matty, Miss Deborah and Mary Smith watch from their window as Captain Brown and his daughters arrive to occupy the small house across the street.

who every Monday night casts up the household accounts and makes sure that not a penny is owed from the previous week. On Tuesday evening, she folds the old household bills and notes into tight spills with which to light the candles. These spills are kept in a wooden box, fixed to the chimney wall. 'Elegant Economy' in practice!

Candles are very expensive and Matty spends a good deal of her time fretting about them. When Mary Smith comes to stay, she notices the many strategies Matty has to use as few as possible. She has taught herself to knit in the dark and keeps the furniture in all the rooms in the same place so that she can find her way round them without having to light a candle to guide her. When Mary, straining to stitch by firelight, asks if she might light a candle, Matty urges her 'to keep blind man's holiday'. That is, to sit in the dark.

Usually candles are lit when tea is brought in but, though there are two candlesticks on the mantelpiece, only one candle is burnt at a time, unless there are visitors. It is important to give the impression that two candles are always lit, so it requires some contrivance to keep them of the same length, ready to be lighted as visitors arrive. Thus, Matty's eyes are habitually fixed on the lit candle, ready to jump up and extinguish it and to light the other before they become too uneven in length. When guests are expected, the ladies stand dressed in their best, each with one of Matty's homemade spills in her hand, ready to dart at the candles as soon as the first knock is heard.

Mary Smith

Mary Smith, a young woman in her early twenties, is now a frequent visitor to the Jenkyns' house. Her mother grew up in Cranford and was a dear friend of Deborah's and Matty's, and of Miss Pole and Mrs Forrester too. On her marriage, she moved to live with her husband in Manchester and Mary was born there. But Mary's mother died when she was young. Her father subsequently remarried a much younger wife and they had several children in short order. Mary's stepmother, Clara, is keen to see her married and takes an active role in bringing this about, much to Mary's distress. After her mother died, Mary first kept in touch with the Jenkyns sisters by letter. Deborah wrote in a rather masculine style, employing 'rolling three-piled sentences' and everything in her letters was

'stately and grand, like herself'. Matty wrote nice, kind, rambling letters, now and then 'venturing an opinion of her own'. It was hers, in spite of a little bad spelling, which were more likely to give a vivid account of what was happening in Cranford.

During one of Mary's visits, Miss Deborah had decided to buy a new carpet for the parlour. Oh, the busy work that Matty and Mary had in keeping the sunbeams off this new carpet, for Deborah was very keen that it should be well protected from both light and feet. They spread sheets of newspapers where the sun shone on it but, within a quarter of an hour, the sun had moved and was blazing away on a fresh spot. Then they had to get down on their knees and shift the position of the newspapers. Deborah was to give a small party in Mary's honour and she set Matty and Mary to stitching together pieces of newspaper, so as to form little paths to the chairs set out for each visitor to prevent their shoes from 'defiling the purity of the carpet'.

Mary suffers the humiliation of her stepmother's match-making plans during the garden party at Hanbury Court.

The Moral Arbiter

Deborah has strong opinions on everything and is used to having people defer to her. She 'had always been the more decided character' whereas Matty in general is so undecided that 'anybody might turn her round to their way of thinking'. Deborah lays down the rules and others follow. Mary finds it astonishing how 'such people carry the world before them by the mere force of their will' but, though she describes herself as 'indiscreet and incautious', she is never inclined to challenge Miss Deborah on any of her pronouncements. When Mary brings oranges as a gift, Matty becomes anxious that Mary may be about to make a hole in hers with her thumb and suck out the juice. She quietly informs Mary that her sister does not approve because it has 'unpleasant associations with a ceremony frequently gone through by little babies'. Deborah does not care for the expression 'suck'. She instructs that they will each choose an orange and repair to their rooms to consume the fruit in solitude. Mary meekly obeys.

Miss Deborah rules that oranges are only to be consumed in the solitude of the bedroom.

Deborah abhors the idea of the railway coming to Cranford. She agrees with Lady Ludlow that allowing the working classes to move more easily around the country will lead to a breakdown of law and order. She fears the migrant labour that would be brought in to raze the land and lay the tracks. It is these strong feelings, when her friend Captain Brown tells her that he is to be Head of Works for the proposed railway line into Cranford, that lead to her sudden collapse and death.

Things change abruptly for Matty. Mary realises that Matty has never even made a decision about a new gown before and now she must rule on all things domestic. She tries to do this by exactly emulating Deborah's way of doing things. She instructs Martha to hand the vegetables to the ladies before the gentlemen. Martha, plain-spoken as ever, says she'll do as told, even though she 'likes lads the best'. Matty reminds Martha that she is forbidden by the articles of her engagement to have a 'follower'.

Panic

After Deborah's death, Mary often comes to stay with Matty and is most fortunately there when Cranford is struck by an apparent 'crime wave'. Dr Harrison's kitchen window is broken one night and a leg of mutton is taken. Rumours of an influx of villains into Cranford spread quickly, fuelled by Miss Pole's vivid recounting of an encounter at her door with a poor gypsy and her starving baby. Panic spreads and Miss Pole ends up taking refuge that night at Matty's house. She is put to sleep, with her silver bundled up in bed with her, in Mary's room.

The idea of a 'crime wave' is set in motion when Dr Harrison and his housekeeper Mrs Rose are disturbed in the night by the sound of breaking glass.

Mary, sharing with Matty, is surprised when Matty rolls a rubber ball under her bed and waits to see that it comes out on the other side before climbing in. Matty explains that she has always had a great dread of hands from under the bed grabbing her by the ankle. To avoid this, she devised a way of taking a flying leap from a distance, but this had annoyed Deborah who prided herself on getting into bed gracefully. So, instead, Matty has adopted the habit of ball-rolling to check no man is under her bed. Mary confesses she has a fear of eyes peering out at her from wooden surfaces. That night they decide it might be best to keep the candle burning.

Crisis

Soon after their father's death, Deborah had decided, against all advice, to invest the entirety of their money in the Town & County Bank, a joint-stock bank that was notoriously unstable. Many years later, the bank crashed and Matty was ruined. She had to receive this shocking news in public, when she was amongst the crowds gathered to see the new summer fashions at Johnson's Stores. It was market day and some of the farmers, having sold their goods, had come in, shyly sleeking down their hair, feeling out of place amongst the ladies and lively prints, but nevertheless anxious to take back home some small part of this gaiety to their families.

Jem Hearne, who had arrived in Cranford as a journeyman from Bolton, was now the town's principal carpenter. He was purchasing a shawl for Martha, but Mr Johnson had refused to accept the five-pound note with which Jem had tried to pay, announcing that any note drawn on the Town & County Bank was now worthless. Matty, with uncharacteristic decidedness, had stepped in and insisted on exchanging her five sovereigns for the note. She said she didn't pretend to understand business but she felt responsible and that it would only be common honesty, as a shareholder, to make good the money. 'I'm loth to make another lose instead of me; five pounds is a deal of money.'

That evening she discovers that she will have but five shillings a week to live on and tries to face it bravely: 'Many a poor person has less and I am not extravagant,' but she sadly accepts that she cannot afford to keep on her maidservant. Martha, however, has ideas of her own. 'I'm never going to leave Miss Matty. I told her so. No! not even if she gives me warning every hour in the day!' She decides that Jem Hearne will marry her and they will support Miss Matty as her lodgers. After a bodily struggle, she drags a reluctant Jem 'all crimson with shyness' in front of Miss Matty.

∞

Jem to Martha: 'You've taken me all on a sudden, and I didn't think to get married so soon – and such quick work does flabbergast a man. It's not that I'm against it, Miss Matty, only Martha has such quick ways with her, when she takes things into her head; and marriage nails a man. I'm a bit fluttered by being pushed straight ahead in matrimony. I daresay I shan't mind it, once it's over.'

Miss Matty and Mary throw rice to celebrate the marriage of serving maid Martha to town carpenter Jem Hearne.

Jem seems to be finally reconciled to marriage on his return with his bride from their wedding.

Change

Mary ponders how Matty will support herself on so little money and considers whether teaching might fit the bill, as that would at least 'throw her among the little elves in whom her soul delighted'. But what could she teach? She has no musical skills and her eyes are no longer good enough to discover the number of threads in a worsted-work pattern. She excelled in knitting garters using a variety of elaborate stitches, the gift of a pair of which had so delighted Mary that she said she was quite tempted to drop one on the street so it might be admired. But this little joke had so distressed Matty's sense of propriety that she had given up this occupation entirely. When reading, Matty always coughs when she comes upon a long word and, though she writes well and with a delicate hand, her spelling is very out-of-the-way. So Mary rules out reading and writing, and concludes that all Matty could teach the young of Cranford is 'patient humility, sweetness and quiet contentment'.

Miss Matty delights in teaching baby Tilly how to water the sunflowers.

Eventually, with the help of Jessie and Captain Brown, Matty is persuaded to open a tea-shop in her dining parlour and, though at first anxious about 'going into *trade*', she turns out to be a successful and resourceful businesswoman. It is during this time that her beloved brother, Peter, returns from India to live with her, and Martha gives birth to a daughter she names Matilda, in honour of Miss Matty. Tilly is 'the child in the house' that Matty has always dreamed of having since she was a young woman on the verge of marriage to Thomas Holbrook. She is at the centre of a busy household and her happiness seems secure. But it is the nature of things to change and Matty's life fractures in the most dreadful way when Martha dies in childbirth along with her second child. Jem, seeing no future in Cranford, packs up and takes Tilly to live with his family in Bolton. Matty is devastated, but she has long since learned to bear grief with fortitude and to burden no one else with her sorrows.

With the younger generation deserting Cranford to take up work opportunities elsewhere, it is not for herself that she is troubled but for the town itself. She fears it will wither at the root and, against all her natural inclinations, she determines to encourage her friends to examine the idea of embracing the future with a more open mind. It is a strange thing, for

Miss Matty,
disturbed that the
young people are
leaving Cranford,
writes to all her
friends, urging them
to reconsider their
opposition to the
railway.

Dear Friends,

My sister was fond of a maxim from the bible ~ "Examine all things. Hold fast to what is good." She was a woman of quite vigorous opinion, and set the pattern for our small society. Her abhorrence of the railway was very widely known, and we all supposed that it was nothing but a menace. However change, or it's refusal, is not within our gift. The young grow apace about us all the time. They desire progress, they are turned to face the sun. And if

it was always thought that Deborah was the stronger of the two Rectory sisters, and yet it was she who could not adapt to the new ways of the wider world that were encroaching on Cranford. By being rigid and inflexible, she broke. Without her sister's firm guidance on everything, Matty has had to make decisions by herself, sometimes considerable decisions that have altered the course of the life of the town. As the winds of change blow through Cranford, it is Matty who has learned to bend and not only to survive, but also to thrive.

⊹ Mrs Forrester ⊱

M RS FORRESTER, the widow of Major Forrester, lives in a 'baby-house of a dwelling' just on the edge of the town. The Major fought the French at Waterloo and returned to be doted on as a hero by his kind and gentle wife. The war with France had kept him absent throughout much of their early married life and, by the time of his retirement from military life in 1815, the chance for Mrs Forrester to bear children had passed. This was to be a constant sadness to her, but one she bore stoically and privately.

Their marriage was affectionate and it afforded Mrs Forrester notable status in the small town where men were rather scarce. The Major was affable and the couple enjoyed socialising; they were a popular addition to the Cranford gatherings. So the whole town mourned when the Major was suddenly carried off by influenza. Mrs Forrester was forced to sell their house in the middle of town and move to her present cottage. She missed his lively company and had to learn again how to make shift by herself. She bought an Alderney calf, which she named Bessie, and all her orphaned affection was directed towards the animal. Bessie became as precious as a daughter to the lonely widow, who kept her in the field next to her cottage and smoothed her muzzle each day with a chamois cloth.

Mrs Forrester felt safer keeping the Major's military top boots and hat on display in the hall to give the impression that she did not live alone, in case strangers came to her door. She was especially afraid of French strangers turning up – not an uncommon fear in Cranford at one time. Miss Matty had once worked out a plan to escape a French invasion by moving everyone down into Mr Buxton's salt mines. She thought it would be an ideal environment for salting food to keep them going through the winter, though she did admit that they might become very thirsty.

When Cranford is in the midst of its supposed 'crime wave', Mrs Forrester pays a young lad from a poor family to stay at night to guard her. She lets him wear the Major's over-large hat and he wildly wields the Major's sword, which is almost as tall as he is. But, being tender-hearted, she feeds him so lavishly that he sleeps through each night while she lies awake listening for intruders.

Mrs Forrester, with her bucket and stool, on her way to milk her beloved cow Bessie.

Although now rather poorer and more threadbare than the other Amazons, she gives her share of parties. She is too proud to accept invitations if she cannot return them. Everyone knows that she has to make do with one young girl from the Charity School, but appearances are important and the Amazons all conspire to keep up the impression that Mrs Forrester has not been busy all morning making her own tea-bread. Nor that she has had to carry her own tray into the parlour because the serving girl is too small to manage it. At the appointed time, those on the sofa move their legs aside, the girl kneels down and drags out the laden tray, while Mrs Forrester affects to wonder what surprises they will find there!

She has a much-admired piece of lace that was made in the previous century by nuns from a silent order, which Mrs Forrester feels bestows a special quality on the lace. She is fond of telling the story of when she had left the precious lace to soak in buttermilk (collected that morning from her dear Bessie) and her cat lapped it up, lace and all. Desperate measures were needed; the cat was secured in one of the Major's top boots and Miss Pole administered a dose of tartar emetic. Some time afterwards, the lace reappeared in the boot, was washed and has been worn ever since. Mrs Forrester always starts her story: 'I do not think you can guess where my lace has been;' and, dropping her voice, 'in pussy's inside!'

Miss Pole with bandaged finger after an encounter with her new parrot, and Mrs Forrester clutching a tiger-skin rug; both were unwanted gifts from Peter Jenkyns.

The whole town knows of her affection for Bessie, and so there is great sympathy when she wanders from her field and falls into the lime pit. Captain Brown organises the rescue party and Bessie is safely pulled out. But the poor beast has lost her hair and comes out looking miserably cold and bald. Mrs Forrester is thankful to have Bessie alive but, as Miss Deborah Jenkyns explains, it would not be proper for her to be seen in Cranford like this: 'She is not bald, she is naked!' Captain Brown makes a light-hearted suggestion that Bessie should be dressed in pyjamas. That same day, Mrs Forrester is seen in Johnson's Stores purchasing a vast quantity of grey fabric. The following day, the whole town turns out to see Bessie in her pasture clad in grey flannel pyjamas.

When Miss Matty loses all her savings, the Amazons agree to pledge what they can each afford in a secret way to help her. Mrs Forrester has

so very little on which to survive, but is as keen as any to help her dear friend. She remembers Matty's kindness to her when they were both about one-and-twenty and her mother lay dying. Her father had sent her to sell eggs in the market to pay for medicine and she had passed Matty and Mr Holbrook in the lane. She had tried to pass unnoticed for she saw that Matty was crying and plucking at the petals of the primroses in her hand, as Mr Holbrook pleaded with her. Even though Matty seemed to be in the midst of troubles of her own, she asked so kindly after her mother and held her hands to comfort her. This kindness has never been forgotten.

Mrs Forrester has a prized recipe for bread-jelly, which is given to invalids to help them recover. A bowl of this bread-jelly is the highest mark of favour Mrs Forrester can bestow. Miss Pole once asked her for the secret of this recipe, but received a firm refusal. Mrs Forrester will not part with it while she lives and, after her death, has bequeathed it to Miss Matty Jenkyns.

Having convinced Mrs Rose that Dr Harrison is in love with her, Miss Pole and Mrs Forrester set about dying her grey hair jet black in time for May Day.

⊷ Miss Pole ⊶

I N CRANFORD, it is impossible to live in the town a month 'and not know the daily habits of each resident'. Most of the collecting and disseminating of this information is due to the tireless work of Miss Octavia Pole.

Each morning, Miss Pole is in the habit of hastening down King Street, 'demurely popping hither and thither into all sorts of places to gratify her curiosity on any point'. In the various shops she investigates new articles on display, but rarely makes a purchase – as many a disgruntled shopkeeper will affirm. For the purpose of these ramblings is not to shop, but rather 'to collect all the stray pieces of intelligence in the town'. Miss Pole takes the self-appointed role as town reporter seriously, and attacks her morning rounds with great singleness of purpose. In fact, had she 'not looked so very genteel and prim', she might have been considered 'impertinent'. (It is rumoured that Mr and Mrs Johnson once privately called her something more than 'impertinent' after she had quizzed them vigorously on the reason they had mysteriously closed the store for two days.)

Such is Miss Pole's acuity and perception that she does not confine her reportage to simple facts. Her friends regard her as 'a kind of prophetess, with the knack of foreseeing things before they came to pass – although she did not like to disturb her friends by telling them of her foreknowledge'. To these great skills, she adds still more, being also an expert on the subjects of children, health and the French, amongst many others.

As Miss Pole's income is a small one, she has but one maid-of-all-work, Bertha, whom she plucked out of the local Charity School at the age of thirteen. She is an industrious and able girl, though wont to offer her own opinions far more than Miss Pole wants to hear them. When Bertha tries to tell her that the cage for her parrot Polly-Cockatoo is in fact a lady's underskirt, Miss Pole firmly puts the girl in her place. (Bertha said she didn't care if she was whipped, for she knew what she knew.) For all that, the two make shift together, and Miss Pole's confidence in Bertha's ability is such that she is kind enough to lend her to her friends in need; though Bertha questions the 'kindness' of this arrangement when it is she who must work the extra hours without prospect of extra pay.

'Miss Pole always had a great deal of courage and savoir faire.'

Old Friends

A childhood friend of Miss Matty's, Octavia Pole was an energetic and sociable girl who lived for the dance season in her youth. An able and lively dancer (with a figure that 'caused no little comment' amongst the young men), she passed many a happy evening in the Assembly Rooms, enjoying the favours of no man in particular, though dances with the flirtatious Peter Jenkyns were the most enjoyable ones of all.

Like many of her friends, she would have liked to marry but a proposal never came her way. Intelligent and self-sufficient, she refused to mourn her fate, and settled into a small residence on Princess Street, a short walk from her dear friend Matty, and chose to wear the badge of spinsterhood with pride. So much so that as the years progressed she claimed to be increasingly baffled as to why a woman should choose to marry at all.

Whenever gossip relating to a married woman comes her way, Miss Pole offers a long congratulation to Miss Matty that 'so far they had escaped marriage, which she noticed always made people credulous to the last degree; indeed, she thought it argued great natural credulity in a woman if she could not keep herself from being married'. But this subject still has

One of the social highlights of the week is the Sunday service, with the Amazons taking their accustomed place in the pew at the front.

the power to rankle when she is with a woman who has married. Indeed, it is one of the few subjects that can lead to an exchange of caustic words with the widow Mrs Forrester, whom Miss Pole believes is often out to 'trounce her' because she has been married and even claims to have enjoyed it! She is particularly wounded by Mrs Forrester's remark that 'when one has known affection' one is more apt to feel its loss in the future. Naturally, Miss Pole refuses to gratify her friend by showing any hurt feelings.

However, Miss Pole is not immune to the pleasures of gentle flirtation. Peter Jenkyns is a favourite amongst the ladies of Cranford, and Miss Pole eagerly vies with her friends for 'who should admire him most'. And after Miss Pole encounters Signor Brunoni at the Assembly Rooms, the *frisson* of that encounter leaves her, unusually, at a loss for words.

She would most certainly want it noted that she possesses a boldness that none of her friends can match. Who was it that ascertained that whiskey is the appropriate drink for a Scottish lady, and was brave enough to first address that lady? ('And has her ladyship been recently *"at Court"*?') And who dared to investigate the secrets of Signor Brunoni's Magic Show?

The fact that Polly-Cockatoo was a present from Peter Jenkyns might explain why the parrot is treated with the greatest care and respect.

Even when she is faced with shocking news, Miss Pole prides herself on keeping her wits about her. When her friends can only stand in mute shock as Lady Glenmire is carried over the threshold by her adoring groom, Miss Pole is inspired to interview the cart driver and within minutes has ascertained all the facts – where they were married, who witnessed it, and what Lady Glenmire wore; this latter piece of information is particularly devastating, as it occurs to Miss Pole that she had been the one to help Lady Glenmire choose the blue velvet tippet, unaware of its intended purpose.

A Question of Loyalty

One might be puzzled why Miss Pole is so deeply wounded by this, but the reason is simple: to Miss Pole, loyalty in friendship matters above all else. When news reaches her that Mr Holbrook is gravely ill, she accompanies Miss Matty to Woodley on that sad visit to say goodbye. And later, when Mr Holbrook's possessions are auctioned after his death, Miss Pole purchases a silhouette of him as a young man as a memento for Matty. And when the distressing news reaches her that Miss Matty's bank has failed and she has lost all of her savings, Miss Pole is the one who speaks to each of the Amazons and proposes a scheme whereby they will all secretly contribute an annual amount to save Miss Matty from penury. That these ladies do so when they have so very little to live on themselves is a testament to their loyalty and friendship. But as Miss Pole says to the assembled company, it would be not only a duty to come to the aid of their dear friend, 'it would be a pleasure'.

The silhouette of Mr Holbrook as a young man, which Matty has kept on her bedroom mantel-shelf ever since Miss Pole secured it for her at the auction after his death.

Miss Pole attends to her crochet while on a visit to her cousin Thomas Holbrook's house. Aware of the sorrow Matty felt over her broken courtship with Mr Holbrook many years before, Miss Pole is instrumental in manoeuvring her to accept his invitation to luncheon. Though personally unimpressed with cousin Thomas's upkeep of the house – she feels he has fallen into 'uncouth habits' by living alone – Miss Pole keeps most of her opinions to herself, knowing that the day belongs to her dear friend Matty.

The Tomkinson Sisters

ANYONE WHO visits Johnson's Stores on a given Saturday will invariably find two sisters idly perusing the latest pattern books and haberdashery. The elder sister, Augusta Tomkinson, might hazard a casual opinion of a particular style or fine piece of silk only to be rebuked by the younger one, Caroline, who claims to have the better taste because she dotes 'on the beautiful and artistic in life'.

This exchange may suggest that Miss Augusta Tomkinson has the more undecided character of the two, but this is not her reputation in the town. Most people regard her as 'brusque and plain-spoken', for she 'piqued herself on her decision of character and sincerity of speech'. When Dr Harrison is first introduced to her, he is not sure that his attentive and protective manner is necessary, as Miss Tomkinson does not strike him as 'remarkably requiring protection from any man'. Relations with her are not improved when he mistakes Caroline for her daughter rather than her sister.

Dr Harrison can be forgiven for his blunder, for Caroline is younger by twenty years 'and so considered as a child by Miss Tomkinson'. Their mother had died soon after Caroline's birth and Augusta, though just a young woman herself, had taken on the vacated role as mother to the baby. She was by nature practical and unsentimental, which was just as well for, with such great responsibilities at home, there was little likelihood of her marrying. When Augusta's father died some years later, he left her with a comfortable house, a modest income and a six-year-old child to bring up.

Augusta took upon herself 'every difficult arrangement, and denied herself every pleasure, and made every sacrifice' in order that her young sister might not feel unsettled by their loss and change in circumstances. In this endeavour Miss Tomkinson was unequivocally successful. Having never known her own mother, Caroline was happy to consider her sister as such, and accept all the attention that was lavished on her. For 'if she was considered as a child, she was also petted and caressed, and cared for as a child'. If something displeased her, her countenance would cloud over

'Miss Caroline was the younger sister by twenty years, and so considered as a child by Miss Tomkinson.'

and she would display a fiery shortness of temper. In anyone else, such behaviour would have warranted a sharp rebuke from Miss Tomkinson, but in Caroline it was forgiven and the cause remedied as quickly as could be.

When the sisters agree to have a new gown apiece for the Hanbury Garden Party, Caroline's heart becomes set on a dress pattern overflowing with 'flounces', requiring a great quantity of silk for its making. Knowing both cannot be afforded, 'Miss Tomkinson gives up her gown to have the whole made up' as her sister wishes, and chooses to wear 'an old, shabby affair herself as cheerfully as if it were Genoa velvet'.

Though not short of money, she is strict with herself in all areas of personal and household expenditure – measures that have in time enabled her to amass a sizeable dowry for Caroline. For Miss Tomkinson had perceived that her sister longed for marriage in a way that she herself never had, and she tries as best she can to plan for it. But with no suitor in sight, and Caroline's thirtieth birthday come and gone, a husband seemed to be the one thing Miss Tomkinson could not secure for her.

It is hardly surprising then that the arrival in town of a handsome young doctor would cause Caroline to swoon and set her sights on him; nor remarkable that Miss Tomkinson should try to tempt him with the offer of the dowry. Nor does anyone consider it unusual for Caroline to collapse on May Day when she discovers that Dr Harrison's heart does not belong to her, as she had been led to believe, but to Sophy Hutton. What does startle everyone is the speed with which Caroline recovers from this heartbreak and engages herself to the town's wealthy butcher, who has been recently widowed and left to care for infant twins. It is the state of being married, Miss Tomkinson realises, that is all-important to her sister. And so by midsummer, she is hosting an engagement party for Caroline after all, though there is no evidence of 'Elegant Economy' on that occasion.

A New Role

Over the following year, Miss Tomkinson must adapt to living on her own for the first time in her life. Even for such a self-sufficient woman it is a great change, particularly enduring the long winter evenings alone. Perhaps it is this loneliness, combined with the long habit of caring for her sister, that explains Miss Tomkinson's willingness to embrace the role of grandmother to Caroline's step-twins. For Caroline, expecting a child

herself, needs her sister's help more than ever. Most days of the week, Miss Tomkinson can now be seen leading the children down King Street (or, as Miss Pole is apt to remark, the children can be seen leading Miss Tomkinson down King Street). If she has timed her walk well, she will run into her dear friend, Matty Jenkyns, playing the same role with little Tilly Hearne. This adds a new dimension to their friendship and a new focus to their lives. Miss Pole is baffled by their keenness to take on the business of child-rearing at their stage of life, though she has no shortage of sage advice to offer them on the subject.

And so Miss Tomkinson prepares to assist at the birth of Caroline's first child. Dr Harrison has been written to for advice. Miss Pole has prepared vast quantities of fresh linens and promised the assistance of her maid, Bertha. Mrs Forrester has presented a tonic for the nerves that she has brewed from motherwort, and Matty has offered her services to entertain the twins during the labour. Galvanised by the support of her friends, Miss Tomkinson looks forward to this new chapter in her life with eager anticipation.

'Dr Harrison advises a bandage – on the abdomen.' Miss Tomkinson reveals the latest developments on her sister's confinement to Miss Matty and Miss Pole.

The Honourable Mrs Jamieson

ITHIN the Amazons' set, it is tacitly understood that Mrs. Jamieson is the most pompous and tiresome member. She never allows her high social standing to be forgotten, so much so that even Miss Deborah Jenkyns (the accepted moral arbiter of the group) always yields 'the post of honour' to Mrs Jamieson. Their loyalty in friendship enabled them to overlook her more annoying traits, noting to each other that 'our friend Mrs Jamieson is much more phlegmatic than most people', as if this somehow excused her behaviour.

She had begun life as Miss Walker, the daughter of a Governor Walker, and married well, if one defines 'well' in terms of social rank rather than happiness. Her husband was the younger brother of the Earl of Glenmire, and they socialised with country gentry, including the Arleys of Arley Hall, another great house like Hanbury Court in the vicinity of Cranford. While this connection gave Mrs Jamieson a great deal of satisfaction, the marriage itself did not. That her husband caused her 'such uneasiness and drank a great deal' is widely regarded as fact amongst the Amazons. Widowed early and left childless on her husband's death, Mrs Jamieson carries the dubious distinction of having lived more years as a widow than as a wife.

Her stately house reflects her character, sitting as it does proudly aloof from the town on 'a road which had known what it was to be a street'. The main living rooms face a pleasant garden at the back and are elegantly, if somewhat formally, furnished. The chairs for her guests are 'all a-row against the wall' and a disheartening distance from the warmth of the fire. Two small tables exhibit conversation pieces – one 'devoted to literature' on which lie a Bible, a peerage, and a prayer book; the other 'dedicated to the Fine Arts', which displays such items as a kaleidoscope, conversation cards and a 'box painted in fond imitation of the drawings on tea-chests'. It is a curious fact that Mrs Jamieson's comfortable income and fondness for food have no visible effect on the quantity or variety of the refreshments she offers to guests, for 'very delicate was the china, very old the plate, very thin the bread and butter, and very small the lumps of sugar'.

An unhappy and childless marriage followed by a long period of widowhood has left an indelible mark on Mrs Jamieson's character. Her closest companion is her dog Carlo.

Living alone, Mrs Jamieson is 'very much at the mercy of her old servants' and of her butler, Mr Mulliner, in particular. 'An object of great awe' to the Amazons, the butler 'seemed never to have forgotten his condescension in coming to live in Cranford. In his most pleasant and gracious moods he looked like a sulky cockatoo.' Miss Pole often catches sight of him through the front kitchen window, his 'head covered with hair powder, which also extended itself over his coat collar down to his very waist'. Invariably he will be engaged in reading the *St James's Chronicle*. This agitates the Amazons as they share a subscription to the newspaper but, 'in right of her honourableness', Mrs Jamieson always has the first reading of it. When there is a delay in forwarding the latest number, an indignant Miss Pole will exclaim: 'I should like to ask him whether his mistress pays her quarter-share for his exclusive use.' But no one dares to ask him anything.

Mrs Jamieson's sole companion is her treasured dog Carlo, who travels everywhere with her and must be treated like a distinguished guest by all. It is often said that a pet will take on the characteristics of its owner, and this is certainly the case with Carlo. Like his mistress, he loves eating and sleeping and possesses a remarkably *au courant* wardrobe (though it can't be presumed that *this* was Carlo's idea).

Whenever Mrs Jamieson entertains the ladies for cards, she has two jugs brought in with the tea – one full of milk and the other of cream. The first cup and saucer are reserved for Carlo, and Mrs Jamieson likes to tell her assembled guests 'how intelligent and sensible the dear little fellow is; he knows cream quite well, and constantly refuses tea with only milk in it'. Alas, the ladies are not allowed to refuse the milk, and so drink their tea in a begrudging silence, while Mrs Jamieson eats her bread and butter with a 'placid, ruminating expression of countenance, not unlike a cow's'.

For those who were acquainted with Mrs Jamieson during the time of her husband's death, it was observed that the sudden loss of Carlo 'was the greater affliction'. Exhausted from grief, she departs to Cheltenham to recuperate. Whether or not the famed waters of that spa town had an ameliorating effect on her spirits is unclear, but the purchase of a new dog – who was of the same temperament and size as Carlo – most certainly did. And so Mrs Jamieson returned to Cranford with the closest to a spring in her torpid step that any of her friends had ever seen.

New Friends

Indolent by nature, Mrs Jamieson does not encourage visitors, but even she is animated by the prospect of a visit from her esteemed sister-in-law, Lady Glenmire. Now widowed, it is her intention 'to pay Mrs Jamieson a long visit, as she had given up her apartments in Edinburgh and had no ties to take her back there in a hurry'. This is a real feather in Mrs Jamieson's cap and she intends to parade her titled guest round the great houses of the neighbourhood. In order not to compromise this plan, she tells the Amazons that they will not be expected to socialise with her honoured guest. Her friends are deeply wounded by the insinuation that they are not of a suitable social standing to meet Lady Glenmire. Even the intrepid Miss Pole is left speechless. So keenly do they feel the slight, they resolve to snub the pair of them, which they do very successfully, much to the bafflement of the Scottish guest.

'Mrs Jamieson came to insinuate pretty plainly that she did not particularly wish that the Cranford ladies should call upon her sister-in-law.'

It takes a chance meeting with Captain Brown for Lady Glenmire to understand the reason for the Amazons' behaviour. She rectifies it by inviting them to a party on Halloween night. After an awkward start, the ladies are delighted to discover that Lady Glenmire is a down-to-earth

woman, keen on fun and company. Mrs Jamieson surrenders her grand pretence and, with glasses full of Mrs Forrester's famed blackcurrant wine, the ladies become firm friends, and scare each other out of their wits with macabre tales of All Soul's Eve.

Strained Relations

Mrs Jamieson stoically acknowledges the great popularity of her house guest, for she has benefited from Lady Glenmire's enlivening company as much as anyone. But her surprise wedding to Captain Brown is something she refuses to acknowledge. The secrecy of her sister-in-law's actions upsets her less than the fact that she's chosen 'to dash her pedigree upon the stones' by marrying a lowly captain who lives in a house fronting the street! She announces that her relations with Lady Glenmire – and with anyone who acknowledges her – are now at an end. For the first time ever, this tight and loyal group of friends suffers a serious fracture: Miss Matty, Mrs Forrester and Miss Tomkinson approve of the match and attend the new Mrs Brown's wedding party; Mrs Jamieson and Miss Pole, who feels personally slighted by Lady Glenmire's secrecy, do not. So distressed is Mrs Jamieson by the wedding that she 'draws down the blinds of her windows, as if for a funeral'.

Mrs Jamieson suffers considerably for her pride, for she becomes increasingly isolated as the weeks come and go without the relief of visitors or visiting. Miss Matty tries to bring about a reconciliation, and indeed Mrs Jamieson really wishes for one herself, but so entrenched is she in her aversion to Lady Glenmire's marriage that she declines Matty's invitation 'in extremely acid terms'. It takes the charm and skill of Peter Jenkyns to bring about a true reconciliation (a rare event in which a *man* proves to be invaluable). He helps Mrs Jamieson to realise that perhaps it is Lady Glenmire's marital *happiness* that is most upsetting for someone who has never experienced such joy herself. The two ladies are publicly re-introduced by Peter at the Christmas party and 'ever since that day there has been the old friendly sociability in Cranford society' which everyone is thankful for, especially Miss Matty because of her 'love of peace and kindliness'.

'Long mourning has been your portion,' says a sympathetic Peter Jenkyns to Mrs Jamieson. 'It must cost you dear to see Lady Glenmire remarry in such haste.'

❖ Captain Brown ❖

I T WAS ONLY a few days after Captain Brown's arrival in Cranford before the ladies of the town resolved to send him to Coventry. They were already out of kilter over the invasion of their territory by a man. But it was not only his masculine gender that dismayed them; it was the fact that he spoke openly about being poor. And not in a behind-closed-doors whisper, but brazenly 'in the public street! in a loud military voice!' In Cranford, poverty (like death) is not a word to be spoken aloud to ears polite. Yet here is Captain Brown loudly proclaiming to everyone the reason why he has not been able to afford to rent a better house. The Amazons had long since tacitly agreed that it should be assumed that no one of their acquaintance is ever prevented by poverty from doing anything they wish. If someone chose to walk from a party, it was 'because the night was fine, the air *so* refreshing; and not because sedan chairs were expensive'. So they are at a loss to know how to deal with a man who does not appear to understand that poverty is a disgrace.

Captain Brown is a retired army captain on a half-pay pension. His wife has recently died and he has moved with his two daughters to Cranford at the request of Sir Charles Maulver, who had been his commanding officer. They had served together during the Afghan wars and Captain Brown had been awarded the Afghanistan campaign medal when he saved Sir Charles's life during the siege of Kabul. He has been drawn to Cranford by the offer of a job; he has two daughters to support, one of whom is seriously ill and in need of constant care. Sir Charles is a director of the Grand Junction Railway Company and has asked him to be Head of Works for the part of the construction that he hopes will one day bring the railway line from Manchester into Cranford. The little town has petitioned against the railway and negotiations are at a delicate stage, so Captain Brown is urged to keep the details of his job confidential and, consequently, not even his daughters know the reason for their removal to the small house directly opposite that of the Misses Jenkyns.

He is an affable man and one who makes no distinction in his manner of dealing with everyone from all ranks of life. When heavily pregnant Bella Gregson tumbles outside the church, he hurries to help her up.

Captain Brown and his younger daughter Jessie move into the modest house across the street from the Misses Jenkyns.

Miss Deborah considers this an act of Christian kindness. But, when he offers Mrs Gregson his arm and insists on seeing her safely home, the Amazons are scandalised; Bella Gregson is a tinker and he is showing her the same degree of courtesy due to a lady. They wait in vain for several days for him to call on them to apologise. He remains blissfully unaware of this expectation and carries on to all as affably as usual.

Friendship

In spite of these assaults on their social code, Captain Brown becomes indispensable to the ladies of the town. His sound masculine common sense wins them over and he is soon consulted as the authority on all problems domestic. His younger daughter, Jessie, taking care of her dying sister, is overwhelmed by the thoughtfulness of her new neighbours. The ladies cook extra and send part of their dinner covered in a basin for the invalid; lavender is sent to burn to sweeten the sickroom; even the poor of the town leave the youngest vegetables on her step. 'What a town Cranford is for kindness!'

Invited by Miss Deborah to an evening party, Captain Brown at once and quietly assumes the man's role in the room. He fills empty cups and takes round the bread and butter in an easy and dignified manner, and sits down to cards with the ladies with just that correct degree of seriousness required for Preference.

When Major Gordon, a colleague from his regiment, turns up unexpectedly, Captain Brown returns their hospitality by inviting the sisters to join the small party to entertain him. He's a good-looking man of forty, and he speaks with fondness of earlier times spent with the Brown family. Only Miss Deborah spots that there has been 'a history' between the Major and Jessie, though even she does not suspect this had resulted in a marriage proposal, which had been most reluctantly turned down. (At that time Jessie was caring for both her mother and sister.)

Deborah feels this is a relationship to be encouraged and so she urges Jessie to accompany Major Gordon in a duet of 'Loch Lomond'. While he sings in a fine baritone, Jessie, who is not very musical, plays the old piano; and Deborah, who is even less so, beats time out of time with her spoon to help things along. This tactic seems to succeed for, the following day, Major Gordon renews his offer and Jessie happily accepts – that is, until

Miss Pole and Mrs Forrester race across Lady Ludlow's lawns to be first with the shocking news that the railway is to come to Cranford.

Captain Brown invites the town to a meeting where he explains the route the railway will take to bring it into Cranford.

she discovers that marriage would mean an immediate departure for India with his regiment, leaving her father to manage by himself. Major Gordon asks her to choose between them, a choice Jessie feels is between love and duty. Refused a second time, Major Gordon leaves immediately for India without her.

Captain Brown, caught up in his 'secret' railway work, fails to notice her heartbreak, just as he was ignorant of her earlier sacrifice; for Jessie too knows how to keep secrets, and they both feel they must protect the other. When he is called away for two weeks on railway business, he asks Deborah to be responsible for Jessie. Deborah, somewhat taken aback by his direct approach, rather coolly reminds him that neighbourliness is a duty that is always observed in Cranford.

The following night, Jessie's sister dies and Deborah, fulfilling her pledge, takes charge (though this mainly involves issuing instructions to Matty and Mary). She finds herself touched by Jessie's situation, but is horrified when Jessie declares that she will follow her sister's coffin to the church: 'Women do not attend funerals!' When it is clear that Jessie will not allow her sister's coffin to travel unattended, Deborah sits awake all night searching her soul for what is the right thing to do. The next morning, against all conventions that she has upheld, she walks side by side with Jessie behind the coffin. The town is astonished, but Miss Deborah's authority makes it acceptable to them. Change has been effected in Cranford. Captain Brown is so touched by this act of kindness, which must have cost her so much, that he carves her a wooden coal shovel, a thing she has often wished for. Their friendship seems assured.

The truth about Captain Brown's job is finally revealed in the worst possible way at Lady Ludlow's summer garden party, when Miss Pole and Mrs Forrester overhear Sir Charles's news that he has sold part of his land to enable the railway to come directly into Cranford. The flustered ladies immediately seek out Captain Brown for reassurance. He is taken off guard by the outrage of the amassed Amazons. He has been able, at the request of Sir Charles, to keep his railway work confidential but, thus directly approached, he cannot lie. So he reassures them in the best way he knows, by telling them the truth: that the railway *will* come to Cranford sooner or later, that change is inevitable but that progress will bring many advantages as well as adjustments. And he finally tells them that he is to be the Head of Works. The effect on Deborah is intense; she sees it as a

betrayal and declares that their friendship is at an end. On arriving home, Miss Deborah suffers a stroke and dies. It will be Christmas before Matty and Captain Brown, now both bereaved, can meet again as friends.

Adjustments

The following year, Cranford goes through some turbulent times and, because of his job, Captain Brown is often at the heart of this turbulence. The railway company is determined to build the Manchester-to-Chester line and the most direct route involves passing through Cranford. Opinion in the town is split: businesses like Johnson's Stores actively petition for it; carpenter Jem Hearne knows he will have no future there without it; and William Buxton is excited by all the possibilities that the engineering will open up. But the Amazons resist it. They fear the influx of immigrant labour that would be needed to build it and they fear the iron beast itself: it has already been the cause of many deaths. Whilst Lady Ludlow lives, the railway is thwarted by her refusal to sell land and Captain Brown's future hangs in the balance.

His personal life is turbulent too. Less than two years earlier, he had been the lively heart of a loving family of four, on full pay with the army. Now, with his wife and elder daughter dead, and Jessie recently reconciled to Major Gordon, newly married and moved to India, he is alone. There are many times when he and Matty, only yards apart across the street from each other, are both sitting in solitary fashion by their firesides, she with her knitting and he with 'Charles Dickens as my friend'.

Resilient though he is, it is not in his nature to live alone. When he comes to the rescue of Lady Glenmire, it is with the same kindness that he showed to Bella Gregson – a quality that greatly appeals to this equally down-to-earth lady. They are both lively and sociable, inclined to make the best of any situation, and neither places too much importance on social standing. They both thrive in company and so, no longer being young, they see no reason to delay and, with matching energy and sense of purpose, they apply for a Special Licence and get married immediately. This time, though the Amazons are greatly surprised by the suddenness of the event, most of them are not scandalised; they see the marriage of two of their dear friends to each other as something to celebrate. The sands once more shift slightly in Cranford.

After their surprise wedding, Captain Brown ushers his new wife over the threshold of his modest house.

❧ Thomas Holbrook ❧

MR THOMAS Holbrook lives at Woodley, a Tudor farmhouse four miles distant from Cranford on the way to Misselton. It is a place that has escaped untouched for centuries, which suits him very well. He has resisted all domestic changes; he sees no need to install a knocker or a doorbell on the wide front door. In summer it stands open all day; in winter a person might use his fist or stick to summon attention. With the same fiercely independent spirit, he has also resisted any change to his status. As a successful farmer with his own estate, he could have pushed himself into the ranks of the squires, but he has insisted on remaining a yeoman farmer. Indeed, he used to return letters addressed to him as Thomas Holbrook, *Esquire* to the post office in Cranford.

He is a tall, proud man with something of the appearance of Don Quixote. In his younger days, he could easily beat the bounds of his land within the day with his long, vigorous strides. He still thinks nothing of walking the seven miles to Misselton and back to buy a book of Tennyson's poems, but now strides with a stooping gait, his hands behind his back; and he pauses more than was his wont to take delight in the changes of the seasons and, when struck by something in particular, quotes snatches of poetry aloud:

> *'In the Spring a fuller crimson comes upon the robin's breast;*
> *In the Spring the wanton lapwing gets himself another crest.'*

Woodley stands among fields in a quiet and pastoral landscape. The garden is old-fashioned 'where roses and currant bushes touch each other, where the feathery asparagus forms a pretty background to the gilly-flowers and pinks'. To the west side of the house is a large barn and, tucked behind, the cowsheds. Mr Holbrook has twenty-six cows, each one called after a letter of the alphabet, and he knows them all.

There was a time, long ago now, when he had imagined carrying his bride across that wide threshold with the door standing open to them. He had offered to Miss Matty Jenkyns and thought she was inclined to accept him. They had met at an autumn dance in the Assembly Rooms, introduced

Thomas Holbrook 'despises every refinement which has not its root deep down in humanity'.

Woodley has resisted all domestic change for centuries, a state of affairs that suits Mr Holbrook very well.

by Octavia Pole, his second cousin. He was struck by the combination of her modesty and liveliness, and by her soft curls and lovely complexion too. He claimed many dances on her dance card that evening.

He took to walking more often into Cranford on the chance of seeing Miss Matty and, throughout that autumn, even though the busiest time for a farmer, he never missed an Assembly Room dance. He became an occasional caller at the Rectory and befriended her brother, Peter. One time, he brought cherries from his trees and Matty's mother talked of her liking for cherry blossom. The following week, he brought a sapling tree from his farm. Her mother suggested Matty take Mr Holbrook to find the best place in the orchard, and they planted it together.

So winter turned to early spring and the dance season came to an end. Mr Holbrook had a busy time of lambing and they did not meet for several weeks. The next time he could walk to Cranford, he was taken by surprise to see Matty bathing a young child in a tin tub outside a modest cottage. The wife had just given birth to her fifth child and Matty's mother had dispatched her with food and instructions to be of use. He stood some way off and watched her. As she scrubbed, she was telling the child a story of a pig that swam across a wide river and both of them were laughing. It was at that moment that he knew he wanted her for his wife.

Being a straightforward man, he would have liked to ask her there and then, but he walked further down the lane to wait. She was startled when she saw him, though blushes and smiles fought in equal measure on her face. His offer was plainly spoken. She was the Rector's daughter and not yet two-and-twenty, he was a farmer and more than ten years older, but they were well suited and he loved her. He could see that he had taken her by surprise and insisted that she give no answer until she had considered. He walked the mile back to the Rectory by her side and they exchanged news of the past weeks. Stopping by the orchard gate, he asked if he might send an invitation to her mother to visit Woodley with both daughters. She seemed pleased with the idea and he said he would wait to hear from her. Then he shook her hand and, for the first time, called her 'Matty'.

Two weeks later, she sent a note asking to see him on the road some way outside Cranford where one side of the path is higher than the other. As he walked to meet her, he gathered a posy of primroses; he knew well her fondness for them. But when she arrived, she was distracted and her words stumbled over each other, as her fingers plucked at the petals of the flowers. She told him she could not marry him. But, ask though he might, she would not give the reason. He wondered if her sister Deborah, who always received him so coolly, had advised against the match? 'No, no...' she insisted; she had told no one of the offer. He was angry and Matty was distressed that she caused such hurt. That night, she would press the few primroses she later found in her hand between the pages of the family Bible. They had parted badly, neither realising that almost forty years would pass before their next meeting.

The primroses from Mr Holbrook that Matty presses between the pages of the family Bible.

A Second Chance

'Matty – Miss Matilda – Miss Jenkyns! God bless my soul! I should not have known you!' are his first words to her when they unexpectedly meet again at Lady Ludlow's garden party. But he keeps shaking her hand in a way that shows the warmth of his feelings. They speak only briefly before he leaves, and Matty spends the rest of the party in a reverie, until jolted by the news (delivered by Miss Pole and Mrs Forrester) that the railway is

to come to Cranford and shocked by the revelation that Captain Brown
is to be Head of Works. That night, her sister Deborah dies and Matty
enters a six-month period of mourning. Mr Holbrook knows it would be
inappropriate to call on her. At Christmas, he sends a note asking if he
may visit her when spring comes round.

The crocuses are pushing through the ground when Matty receives
an invitation to visit Mr Holbrook, together with Mary and Miss Pole.
Matty sits bolt upright on the journey and looks wistfully out of the
window when they draw near. She has never seen Woodley, the place
that would have been her home. 'It is very pretty,' she whispers almost to
herself. Mr Holbrook is at the open door to greet them, rubbing his hands
in eager hospitality.

As they sit down to lunch, he and Matty agree that they do not like
the 'new-fangled ways' of meals. He explains his father's rule: 'No broth,
no ball; no ball, no beef.' Dinner always started with broth from the boiled
beef, followed by suet pudding. If they were not both eaten, then no beef
was allowed. This day, the beef is served with peas, which causes some

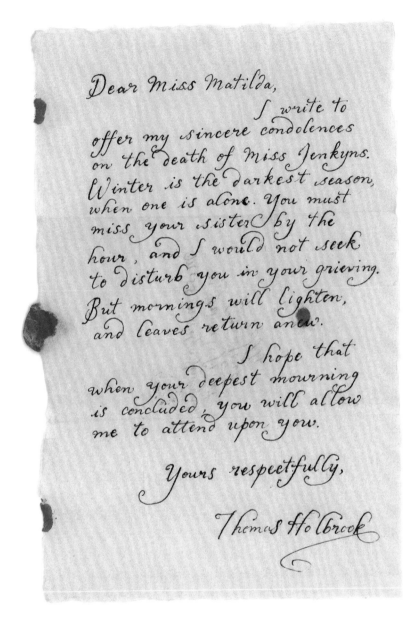

Dear Miss Matilda,
                    I write to
offer my sincere condolences
on the death of Miss Jenkyns.
Winter is the darkest season,
when one is alone. You must
miss your sister by the
hour, and I would not seek
to disturb you in your grieving.
But mornings will lighten,
and leaves return anew.
                    I hope that
when your deepest mourning
is concluded, you will allow
me to attend upon you.

          Yours respectfully,

               Thomas Holbrook

Mr Holbrook writes to Matty at Christmas. When her mourning is over, he will invite her to dine at Woodley.

dismay to the ladies as the forks are the old-fashioned variety with two spaced prongs. Miss Matty picks them up one by one on the point of one prong; Miss Pole sighs and gives up altogether. Only Mary manages. She watches Mr Holbrook shovelling them up wholesale on the round-edged blade of his knife: 'I saw, I imitated, I survived!'

Afterwards, they sit in the counting house, a beautiful book-lined room where Mr Holbrook pays his labourers their weekly wages at a large

At Woodley, luncheon is still conducted in the old-fashioned manner that suits Mr Holbrook, although the ancient cutlery poses problems for the ladies.

oak table by the door, and he asks Matty to fill his pipe for him. Deborah had trained her to abhor smoking, so she hesitates. But she knows this gesture in their youth was always considered a compliment to a lady and, gratified, she daintily packs the strong tobacco into the bowl. He reads aloud 'Locksley Hall', a poem by Mr Tennyson, and, when Miss Pole complains of a draught, it is Matty's shoulders he covers with a shawl.

When Mary privately compliments him on the care he has put into the visit, his reply is simple: 'I've had forty years to plan it.' Later, as he hands the ladies into the carriage, he says that he will call on them soon. On the way home, Matty muses: 'It is very pleasant dining with a bachelor. I only hope it is not improper, so many pleasant things are.'

Matty finds several reasons for wearing her prettiest caps each noon and for standing half hidden watching by the window. On the third day, Mr Holbrook calls bearing a posy of primroses. Matty holds them gently on her lap as they talk, knowing that later she will press them into the same page of the family Bible. Suddenly he announces his intention of travelling to Paris; he's always had a whim to go and means to do so immediately! She is taken aback but, he explains, he does not travel abroad without a reason; he hopes that whilst he is away Matty will take pause to consider how their future path together might lie. She understands. As he leaves, he gives her the book of Tennyson's poems that he had read to her at Woodley and bids her to take care of herself and calls her 'Matty' again, as he did so long ago.

Matty frets while he is away in Paris; she is sure the food will not agree with him. She waits impatiently for his return. On the journey back, he contracts a chill and arrives at Woodley in a serious condition. Miss Pole breaks the news to Matty and they travel to see him, but arrive too late. He has died. Matty sits by him, taking his hand in hers, and remembers the Tennyson he read to her:

> *'Cursed be the social wants that sin against the strength of youth!*
> *Cursed be the social lies that warp us from the living truth!*
> *Well – 't is well that I should bluster! Hadst thou less unworthy proved*
> *Would to God – for I had loved thee more than ever wife was loved.'*

Mr Holbrook reads Tennyson's 'Locksley Hall' to the ladies, while Matty fills his pipe.

Hanbury Court

ON THE FAR eastern edge of Cranford lies a set of elaborate gates with the crest of the old and noble estate of Hanbury worked elaborately into the ironwork and still just discernible despite the ravages of time and weather. If you were to travel through those gates you would find yourself on a miry lane that cuts across ancient pasture lands for a mile or more before falling gradually down a grassy gorge to the lower land. Here, rows of high elms line both sides, suggesting that in former times this bowery lane was both wider and grander. Honeysuckle grows in wild profusion here, its scent wafting through the air and mingling with that of sweet woodruff, which grows in great drifts in the woodland beyond. Another mile further and the lane cuts across a parkland of a more formal design, with great lawns and ornamental lakes and follies arranged to delight all the senses, before it widens out in front of Hanbury Court, a grand manor house and home to Lady Ludlow, Cranford's reigning aristocrat.

Lady Ludlow is a Hanbury 'of that old stock that flourished in the days of the Plantagenets'. Now an elderly widow, she still maintains a firm hold over her household and the community, though she is guided by ideas that were in vogue during her youth and are now considered distinctly 'singular'. She was a child during the French Revolution, and so was raised on harrowing stories of the savagery meted out to the upper classes by the 'mob'. When she came of age, she fashioned herself as a compassionate autocrat over her tenants and community, believing that this would ensure that no such bloody upheaval ever occurred on English soil.

Public Duties

When Lady Ludlow was just a girl, her father began to teach her how to run the estate, giving her a training that she thought 'unusual in those days'. An intelligent and energetic child, she relished this education and liked to tell how her father would take her with him on his rides, and 'bid her observe this and that, and on no account to allow such and such things to be done'. By and by, when the time came for her to put this education

*Lady Ludlow:
'When I was a girl, one never heard of the rights of men, one only heard of the duties.'*

into practice, she relished her new role and was proud of her personal superintendence of the estate. But her mistrust of change of any kind has ensured that her farms, from which Hanbury derives most of its income, have become less and less profitable as the years have passed.

After several seasons of particularly poor harvests, her land agent Mr Carter urges her to make household economies to compensate for the shortfall but 'if it affected the welfare of others, or the honour and standing of the great house of Hanbury', she was inflexible. So Lady Ludlow refuses to reduce her extensive household staff, a number of whom are invalids, because she feels a responsibility for them and justifiably fears that many would end up in that most dreaded of institutions – the Workhouse. This includes the deaf-mute Will Jones whose sole job is the winding of her many clocks.

Though Hanbury Court sits just two miles from Cranford, it exists as a world of its own.

This intransigence, despite its honourable intentions, leaves them with few options for raising income. The most obvious and lucrative opportunity would be to sell a portion of the estate to the Grand Junction

Railway Company, whose ideal route into Cranford would involve cutting across Hanbury lands. But Lady Ludlow is horrified. She believes that the railway will enable the working classes to move about too freely, which she is certain will stir up social unrest (a view shared by many in Cranford). But she also considers it her sacred duty to protect the estate of Hanbury and pass it on in its entirety to her heir, Septimus.

Across England, the cry for universal education was beginning to be heard, but Lady Ludlow would have none of this. With the spectre of the Reign of Terror ever present in her mind, she found this notion 'levelling and revolutionary'. Moreover, she could not see how formal education would equip the working classes with a moral education, which she values above all else. For that, she tells Mr Carter, all one needs to know is the Creed, the Lord's Prayer and the Ten Commandments, 'which teach simple duties in the plainest language'. But Mr Carter belongs to a younger generation and is guided by his own history. Raised by forward-thinking yeoman farmers, he received an excellent education that allowed him to

Since his wife's death, Mr Carter has lived quietly. That is, until Harry Gregson brings new focus to his life and a determination to secure a better future for him.

be trained as a land agent and move up in the world. When he sees a similar brightness and desire for learning in Harry Gregson, he feels compelled to teach him to read, even knowing that this must be done in secret. Harry becomes the son he never had, and an extraordinary bond grows between them.

To be sure, Lady Ludlow is a traditionalist, but she is not always inflexible. Her tenant farmers are obliged to present their rents to her once a week at midday. Mr Carter realises that this loses them the better part of a working day because they have to stop work, return home to wash and dress in Sunday clothes, and then change again afterwards before resuming work. This gives him a simple idea: let them present their rents before the working day starts. Lady Ludlow sees how this benefits everyone and she changes the centuries-old tradition.

On some things, she seems more resolute. Mr Johnson is assaulted and robbed outside his shop, and Cranford panics. When the notorious local vagabond Job Gregson is seen in town with money to spare, it is assumed that he's the culprit and they arrest him for the crime. If found guilty, he could be transported to Australia, leaving his large family destitute. In fact, Job's money had come from selling prize pheasants he and Harry poached from Lady Ludlow's land that same night. To save his father, Harry must confess his part in the crime and bear the weight of Mr Carter's disappointment in him. Mr Carter tells Lady Ludlow of the wrongful arrest and asks her to intervene to release Job. She is astonished by the request; poaching is still a serious crime and to appear to condone it would set a dangerous precedent. Besides, the Gregsons are not tenants of hers, so she bears no responsibility for the family.

Job Gregson in the Lock-up awaiting sentencing.

But Lady Ludlow remains troubled by this encounter and decides to observe the situation for herself, just as her father had taught her to do. For the denizens of Hareman's Common, it is surely an incongruous sight to witness Lady Ludlow's magnificent coach-and-four making its ponderous way down the deep-rutted lane; more astonishing still perhaps, when the coach pulls up in front of Job's hovel, and a little pair of high-heeled shoes alight from the carriage and make their 'dainty way among the yellow pools of stagnant water that had gathered in the clayey soil'.

When she witnesses the grim reality of Bella Gregson's life with her children, Lady Ludlow takes the unprecedented step of intervening directly with the local magistrate, Sir Charles Maulver. He insists that it is not for them to interfere with the law, but she upbraids him: who makes the laws in England, if not landowners such as Sir Charles and herself in the House of Commons and House of Lords? They have every right to intervene when 'right is on their side' and it affects their own people. It is a remarkable *volte-face* on her part.

Personal Sorrows

Lady Ludlow has long been a widow but her intense grief is not from the loss of her husband, but the deaths of six of her seven children. In her boudoir she keeps a collection of private treasures – exquisitely painted miniatures held inside a locket or bracelet, childish drawings, a broken riding whip and, most poignantly of all perhaps, locks of hair 'carefully ticketed'. Whenever she touches these locks she is filled with melancholy, knowing that they were a part of a beloved child 'she may never touch and caress again'.

Her sole surviving child is Septimus, now in his thirties, whose absence from home is a source of deep regret. After taking his Grand Tour of Europe, he elected to settle in Italy, claiming that it was an ideal climate for his delicate health. No subject could be more alarming to any mother than the health of her last surviving child and so Lady Ludlow has stoically accepted that, for the moment, he must live abroad. To add to her woes, Septimus shows no inclination to marry and, as the years pass, his journeys back home have dwindled. Each year, her heart soars with the hope that the heir of Hanbury will be by her side at the Hanbury Garden Party. And each year, after assuring his mother that he will indeed attend, he fails to appear. This cycle of disappointment has taken its toll on Lady Ludlow's spirits, though only her closest companion, Miss Galindo, knows how much heartache she bears in private.

Sir Charles Maulver with Septimus's companion, Giacomo (right). Sir Charles urges Septimus to follow his lead and sell the Hanbury estate to the railway company.

Mr Carter is not indifferent, but his anger at the ceaseless demands for money from Septimus makes him an unsympathetic listener. Lady Ludlow knows that the Hanbury coffers cannot support these demands but, in a rare moment of weakness, she confesses that she is incapable of saying no to her beloved son. Having thus rejected all advice from Mr Carter, Lady Ludlow heads inexorably towards the last unthinkable option: to take out a mortgage on the estate. After a lifetime of careful superintendence of her lands, this is a terrible blow that robs her of her sleep and peace of mind.

It is witnessing Lady Ludlow's distress over the mortgage that leads Mr Carter to the Railway Works on the fateful day of his accident. Failing to raise funds by selling timber or tools to the railway company, he attempts to put things right in a hastily drawn up Will before he dies. This extraordinary act of generosity and foresight on his part brings these two central people in his life together – Lady Ludlow, the Liege Lady of the town, and Harry Gregson, the son of an itinerant poacher. They both promise to follow Mr Carter's wishes to the letter, and in so doing, the most unlikely of friendships is born.

The Last Generation

When Septimus fails to make an appearance at the garden party the following year, Lady Ludlow falls into a terminal decline. The malignancy in her bones is so severe that Miss Galindo writes to Septimus urging his immediate return. Lady Ludlow insists on waiting for him up to her last breath in the Great Hall, standing to welcome the heir back to Hanbury. Though her will remains iron-strong, her body cannot withstand the long wait. She dies before he arrives. Septimus's grief, remorse and nostalgia prove a heady concoction, and he makes the unexpected announcement that he intends to honour his forebears by remaining at Hanbury and taking up his role as head of the estate.

But, as soon as Septimus reads his mother's Will and realises that the farms will always struggle to be profitable, he decides to sell Hanbury to the railway company. He packs up the many treasures accumulated by his ancestors, dismisses the staff and closes up the house. He will return to Italy, a much richer man. As his carriage drives past the shuttered house, it bears the last Ludlow ever to see Hanbury. It is the end of an era.

Lady Ludlow interviews Harry in the Great Hall. The most unlikely of friendships will be born out of their mutual regard for Mr Carter and the unique legacy he leaves them.

Septimus attempts to cheat Harry by falsely claiming that full repayment of the loan he made to Lady Ludlow will bankrupt the estate and result in the dismissal of all household staff.

Miss Galindo &
Harry Gregson

LAURENTIA Galindo has resided in a tiny cottage on King Street for many years, keeping house on the 'smallest possible means', yet always managing to maintain a servant. And this servant was invariably chosen because she had some infirmity that made her 'undesirable to every one else' – such was Miss Galindo's character.

The daughter of a baronet, she was orphaned at the age of eleven and came to live with distant relations, the Ludlows at Hanbury Court, where she was brought up alongside Septimus and Lady Ludlow's other children. Although she was treated as one of the family, she was determined to lessen the burden of herself on the household. She had always been skilled with her hands and she started to make her own clothes. She showed such flair with hats that even Lady Ludlow was seen wearing them.

When she came of age, with no inheritance with which to support herself, she had to cast about to find a means of making a genteel living. Millinery seemed the obvious choice, and even though it counted as *trade*, she was fortunate to have the enterprise sanctioned by Lady Ludlow, whose blessing would guarantee a discerning clientele. And so each weekday morning from nine o'clock until noon, Miss Galindo transforms her tiny parlour into a showroom – bringing out a set of folding mirrors and displaying a number of samples on stands.

The Amazons are dependable and enthusiastic habitués of her shop, though not its ideal customers. As they are all as poor as Miss Galindo, 'Elegant Economy' must extend to all matters of dress and so many more hats are tried on than will ever be purchased. Their tendency to shop en masse and to speak over one another often leads to pandemonium in that tiny parlour, which takes on an aviary-like atmosphere during their visits. Miss Galindo sometimes struggles to keep her 'peppery temper' in check during these invasions and finds that a quick pinch of snuff taken in the back room helps tremendously with this. The Hon. Mrs Jamieson is her best customer, but her patronage comes at a price. She always insists that her dog Carlo is offered milk and biscuits, and, when a new purchase is decided upon, that Miss Galindo must fashion a matching one for him.

Miss Galindo's aristocratic background, reserved nature and her employment in trade make it difficult for her to fit in socially with any one group in the community – a circumstance which she bears with admirable stoicism.

Harry's intellectual curiosity and pluck bring him to the attention of Mr Carter, who can see beyond his reputation in town as 'half gypsy and whole poacher'.

Miss Galindo's reserved and self-sufficient character wins her respect amongst the ladies of the town, but few friends. She is confidante to Lady Ludlow and a regular visitor to Hanbury but, given their differences in age and status, it cannot be a friendship of equals. When Lady Ludlow decides that Miss Galindo will assist Mr Carter with his paperwork, she cannot decline even though, by taking time away from her millinery work, it means a loss of valuable income. Certainly, she does not attempt to hide her peppery temper from Mr Carter when she discovers that his need for a clerk is a ruse. They both initially resent the arrangement but gradually a warm friendship develops. They share a mutual respect and compassion for both Lady Ludlow and Harry Gregson and, as two intelligent but lonely people, they begin to take pleasure in each other's company for its own sake. Alas, this budding romance is cut tragically short by the untimely death of Mr Carter and Miss Galindo finds herself as clerk and witness to his Will, which surprisingly bequeaths his entire fortune to Harry.

On the margins of existence, with an itinerant and unreliable father, Harry has been forced to take responsibility for his large family from an early age.

A life of grinding poverty has made Harry remarkably resilient and self-sufficient. At an early age he learned to poach – fish, rabbits, birds – as a necessity of survival. By the time of his tenth birthday, he has taken on the responsibility of feeding his family, a grim milestone that is marked by his father with the gift of a pair of second-hand boots – the first time Harry's feet have been shod. But he is a bright and curious boy and the scrap of newspaper that the boots are wrapped in catches his attention; he can recognise some of the words! His mother is pleased, but Job warns him fiercely that learning is not for the likes of him. Lady Ludlow reacts in the same way when she learns that Mr Carter has been teaching him to read. She offers Harry a permanent job in her cattle sheds, a sure means to support his family. The price? He must give up the idea of an education.

When Mr Carter dies, Harry and Miss Galindo both lose their closest friend. Harry is deeply grateful for the formal education Mr Carter secures for him in his Will, but he soon discovers that fulfilling his mentor's wishes is much harder in practice. He is different from the other boys at Shrewsbury School and so he is bullied. Harry soldiers on until he can bear it no longer, then he runs away. But he returns to discover

his family evicted because of the Railway Works and that his father has set up as an itinerant knife-grinder and taken the family on the road.

For a time, both Harry and Miss Galindo lose their way in a world that is changing for them. Miss Galindo struggles in the role thrust upon her as surrogate mother and fails at first to appreciate the extent of Harry's unhappiness. Effectively orphaned at a vulnerable time in life, Harry is angry and increasingly rebellious, particularly when he's told he must return to school. But, after Miss Galindo comes to understand Harry's desperation, she realises that what Harry needs to thrive is a new school and a new home life. With this realisation, comes one about herself; her life in Cranford has become intolerably lonely since the deaths of Mr Carter and Lady Ludlow. And so she and Harry decide to embark on a new stage of their lives together. They will move to Manchester where Harry can attend the grammar school and Miss Galindo can take a house nearby in which they will live as a family. With a renewed sense of hope, Harry revives the dream he and Mr Carter shared for his future – to build the first school in Cranford, where he will become its first teacher.

Though she at first considers him a thorn in her side, Lady Ludlow ultimately comes to respect Harry for his integrity and honest nature.

❖ Dr Harrison ❖

'ONCE UPON a time, a gallant young bachelor was sorely puzzled where to settle when he had completed his education as a surgeon.' The name of this kind-hearted and energetic doctor was Frank Harrison. The town he settled on was Cranford.

It is a little-known fact that before he received a particular letter from an old cousin of his father's, Frank had never heard of that fine town. Indeed, on finishing his training at Guy's Hospital in London, he took a fancy to going abroad and thought of offering himself up as a ship's surgeon. But then Dr Morgan wrote with an attractive proposal: this gentleman was a doctor with a 'capital country practice' and, as he was getting on in years, he wanted to take on a young partner who could, in time, take over the practice in full. He proposed giving Frank a third of the profits for the first five years, and then half of the profits thereafter (until the elder doctor's eventual retirement). It was a handsome offer, particularly for a penniless young man with no social connections, and he readily accepted it.

On his arrival, Dr Morgan sets about promoting his protégé in Cranford, calling first on Miss Deborah Jenkyns, whose good opinion, if bestowed, would set the tone for the town. She is rather alarmed by the new doctor's lack of years and the fact that he 'trained in *London!*' She fears he might try to introduce new-fangled medical notions into Cranford, and believes she represents all the ladies when she declares that they are a robust community and have fared perfectly well with their own kitchen physic for most ailments, calling out Dr Morgan only *in extremis*. Sensing opposition to his plan, canny Dr Morgan resorts to Miss Pole. He mentions casually that, whilst at Guy's Hospital, Frank had been tutored by the eminent surgeon Sir Astley Paston Cooper. (The truth was that Frank had merely attended two of Sir Astley's lectures.) Miss Pole immediately sets to work reporting this extraordinary piece of intelligence and, by nightfall, it has become established *as fact* that Sir Astley had assisted Dr Harrison in 'his duties as surgeon to the Royal Family'.

With this distinguished pedigree, Dr Harrison sets up his practice in Cranford, in a house he rents on King Street. Jem Hearne is employed to build folding doors to divide the large sitting room: the front parlour will

Dr Harrison arrives in Cranford in his newly purchased 'Cutaway' coat. Appalled by this latest fashion from London, Dr Morgan instructs him to wear black – the only trusted colour of their profession.

Mary Smith and Dr Harrison become firm friends after admitting they are not romantically attracted to one another. When Dr Harrison reveals that he has fallen in love with Sophy Hutton, Mary offers encouragement.

Dr Harrison attempts to save Mr Carter's life after he is gravely injured in an explosion at the Railway Works.

be used as his dining room and the back half will serve as his consulting room. Having as yet no money, he has no possessions, apart from his old nursery chair and his books. But Dr Morgan offers a skull for the top of his bookcase and advice that he should keep the novels of Miss Austen 'with their backs turned to the wall' in case he is thought frivolous.

Dr Morgan also arranges a housekeeper, the recently widowed Mrs Rose, whose husband was a 'brother surgeon in a neighbouring town' and whose 'smattering of medical knowledge' Dr Morgan thinks will be invaluable. Frank finds it 'rather queer to be the master of this house with another person's furniture', but Mrs Rose proves to be as kind and attentive as Frank and they settle into their new way of life together.

But soon Dr Harrison and Dr Morgan find themselves at odds over a medical matter. When Jem Hearne falls from a tree and suffers a compound fracture of his arm, Dr Morgan believes that amputation is the only answer. Frank believes he can save the arm, and advocates a newer treatment. But he confesses that he has never performed this procedure himself; he has only watched the operation in medical school. While admitting that there is risk attached, Frank refuses to bend to pressure from Dr Morgan. The town is riveted by this quarrel and it becomes a very public test of his skills and courage. When the treatment proves successful, Dr Harrison secures not only Jem's working livelihood and gratitude, but his own reputation in the town. At least, for the time being.

The Fairer Sex

Dr Harrison soon discovers that treating the ailments of the fairer sex is by far his greatest challenge. Dr Morgan tutors his protégé in the specific ways of the Cranford ladies – lessons he must learn if he expects his practice to flourish. He is advised to 'acquire an attentive, anxious politeness, which combines ease and grace with a tender regard and interest'. He reminds Frank that the female sex rely upon them for kindness and protection. A friendly and sympathetic fellow by nature, Frank sees no reason to resist this advice, though diagnosis often proves elusive; amongst his younger female patients in particular, curious palpitations of the heart, faintness and loss of appetite seem bafflingly common.

Perhaps if Dr Harrison were more worldly, he might have realised that advice which worked perfectly for 'a fidgety meddlesome old bachelor'

The sending and receiving of Valentine cards causes a flurry of excitement amongst the young hearts in the town, but one mischievously sent to Caroline Tomkinson has grave consequences for Dr Harrison.

could be a recipe for misunderstanding when practised by a handsome and charming younger one. But he had never been 'a clever judge of countenance'. Frank's childhood had been a lonely one; his father died when he was a boy and he grew up alone with a mother who was naturally reserved. When he returned home in the school holidays, he mistook her cool countenance for displeasure at seeing him. She would later tell him that 'the opposite was true', but Frank never gained an instinct for interpreting her expressions – or indeed any woman's. There had been no sisters to teach him and, once he came of age, his socialising was confined to his own sex at Guy's Hospital. He admits that this lack of perception makes him ideally suited to being a doctor as 'patients have only two expressions – pleasure, that you have come to cure them, and fear that you will not'.

When Frank falls in love with Sophy Hutton, he begins to 'think a good deal about money' and wonder if his income of 'three hundred a year, with a prospect of increase' will satisfy Reverend Hutton and allow him officially to court his daughter. When the Reverend consents, Dr Harrison is so elated that he goes about 'on wings instead of feet' and becomes 'universally benevolent, and desirous of giving pleasure to every one'. Unfortunately, this universal happiness is misinterpreted; Mrs Rose and Caroline Tomkinson are both convinced by others that his kind gestures or professional care are signs of love and that an announcement of their betrothal is imminent.

So May Day dawns, with high expectations in many hearts in the town. Dr Harrison's are perhaps the highest of all, for he eagerly anticipates the moment when he will show the town that he is officially walking out with Sophy Hutton. But, as the weather darkens, his hopes are dashed in the most blisteringly public way when he is challenged to declare his engagement to the two other ladies. He is so astonished and baffled by this turn of events that he cannot find the words to exonerate himself. The Rector accuses him of deceit while Sophy, reeling from the devastation and humiliation of these revelations, collapses and is escorted home. It will be many weeks before Frank sees her again, and that will be when she is in danger of dying from typhoid fever. It is his radical treatment of her fever, when all else has failed, that finally restores his reputation in the town and proves his love to Sophy.

Their marriage is sanctioned by Reverend Hutton (and fortunately by the Amazons), and everyone is full of good wishes for the future happiness of the young couple. Frank readily forgives the community for their previous bad opinion of him. It is not in his nature to hold a grudge and he has grown genuinely fond of the town and its inhabitants.

However, as a young and talented surgeon, Dr Harrison longs for medical opportunities unavailable to him in such a small and (as Miss Pole was wont to remind him) inherently 'healthful place'. When he is offered the chief surgical position at the newly opened hospital in Bury, his heart leaps at the opportunity.

The ladies are sorry to see him leave and continue to correspond with him about any illnesses in the town. By and by, though he had lived there but a year, they start to claim him as their own and, whenever he visits with dear Sophy and their children, they are proud to show him off to any newcomers as a 'Cranford man'.

With Sophy fully recovered from typhoid fever, she and Dr Harrison are wed in Cranford church, officiated by the Reverend Hutton and in front of the people of the town.

⊷ The Rectory ⊶

T HE CRANFORD Rectory has been home to many families since it was built in 1526. It started life as a farmhouse on land belonging to a local manor but in 1586, just at the time when Sir Walter Raleigh was arriving back in England with the first tobacco from Virginia, the lord of the manor died without issue, bequeathing all his effects to the diocese.

The farmhouse stood close by the church, which had been built in the late twelfth century by the Knights Templar, and could now serve as its church house. The dark panelling from one room at the manor was stripped out and carried by horse and cart down the rutted lanes, to be fitted over the stone walls of the largest room to make it more appropriate for the men of God who would now live there. Many of these churchmen over the next 250 years, noticing the joins, would remark what a hasty job this must have been. It is a house that needs a family to animate its beauty.

It has been thirty-five years since Matty Jenkyns lived here, but she catches herself now and then still thinking of it as 'home'. Her bedroom had overlooked the garden and she had liked to open the window and sit looking at the changes that each season brought. Now it is Sophy Hutton who sits at the same window and delights in the espaliered Jagonelle pears growing on the warm brick wall, with the neat beds of vegetables abundant beneath them.

It is one of Sophy's jobs to tend the kitchen garden, with the help of her two younger sisters, Lizzie and Helen, and the hindrance of Walter, their six-year-old brother. In truth, Sophy has very few such opportunities to sit and gaze. Although still a year short of twenty-one, she has been the mother to this family since she was Lizzie's age of fourteen. Their mother had died giving birth to Walter, and Sophy had abruptly had to put away childish things and take on responsibilities beyond her years, helped only by Bessie, their maidservant, who was herself still young.

Reverend Hutton's faith is shaken by the loss of his adored wife and, in order to survive this crisis, he insists that it was the will of God and throws himself with renewed vigour into his ministry. He cauterises his grief so successfully that he fails to notice over the years that Sophy

Reverend Hutton. 'He was very quiet and reserved, almost absent at times; he is so dignified – altogether a man you would talk to with your hat off whenever you met him.'

is sacrificing her young life in order to nurture his family and run the household. She has no time for social engagements of her own and once confides to Mary Smith that she fears she will never marry because, by the time Walter is grown enough to be independent, she will be too old to meet anyone.

But Sophy is about to be proved wrong, for a new young man arrived yesterday in Cranford and she is about to meet him. Dr Frank Harrison is accompanying Dr Morgan on his rounds and they arrive at the Rectory to see Bessie, who has a bad knee. Dr Morgan is taken upstairs to attend to the patient and Dr Harrison is instructed to wait in the drawing room.

He pushes open the old wooden door and is instantly captivated by what he sees framed there like a picture: a room of rich colours – sea green and crimson, dark-panelled walls and a low casement window open to the sunny garden, surrounded with white clustered roses whose scent drifts to where he stands, enchanted. Sophy is sitting on a cushion on the carpet, with the sunlight falling from above making her hair look like the spun gold of a fairy tale. Gathered close to her lap is a sturdy, round-eyed little

boy with the same hair colouring and she is teaching him the alphabet: '… and this is a kicking K…' The room is not tidy; there are books and pieces of work about and children's playthings on the floor but, to Frank, everything he sees suddenly makes him understand 'the full charm of the word *home*'. He simultaneously falls in love with the room and with the young woman inside it.

Walter is delighted to have his lesson interrupted and suggests they pick some cherries for their visitor, running ahead of them into the garden, which is heavy with the sound of bees busy in the brilliant flower borders. In the orchard, Sophy takes a rake to knock down the cherries and Frank gazes in wonderment at her upturned throat as she stretches to reach the ripest ones. When he takes the rake and shakes the higher branches, cherries rain down on them all, and Sophy and Walter, laughing, try to catch them in apron and basket.

At this moment, Frank is at the tip-top of bliss and wants to stay here for ever; under this cherry tree, planted all those years ago by Thomas Holbrook and Matty Jenkyns.

Dr Harrison interrupts Walter's reading lesson: 'It was mighty relief to him when I came in, as I could see, and I am much mistaken if he was caught up again to say his lesson.'

Trials

Sophy's life is so proscribed by family duties that she and Frank meet only at church, and so both wake on the morning of the Hanbury Garden Party with keen anticipation of what the day might bring. They will travel all together in the convoy from the town and a day of pleasure seems to stretch ahead. Walter has a little hoarseness and Bessie warns Sophy that he is not fit to go out, but Sophy cannot bear to miss the fun and makes a decision that will torture her for the rest of her life. She looks after him carefully all the afternoon and wraps him in her shawl for the journey home through the mists, but Walter collapses with the croup that night. Dr Harrison is sent for and he and Sophy battle together to save Walter, but to no avail and he dies in Sophy's arms. She blames her selfishness for his death. If she had not been so keen to spend time with Dr Harrison, she would have kept Walter at home. Frank tries to reassure her that she is blameless, but her guilt makes it impossible for her to be in his company and she asks him not to call.

Sophy returns home, already showing the early signs of typhoid fever.

Six months later, when Valentine's Day dawns, the Rectory girls are officially out of mourning and Frank risks sending Sophy a small posy of snowdrops with his compliments. Noticing Sophy's quiet joy, and approving of the doctor's modest and proper gesture, the Rector invites him to join the family on Shrove Tuesday. Here Frank sees another tableau of his 'ideal family', when they gather in the kitchen to cook pancakes together. So loath is he to leave that he continues to eat every pancake put in front of him.

Later that week, Frank asks the Rector for formal permission to court Sophy and he is allowed to drive her, chaperoned of course by her two sisters, to the bluebell woods that edge the Heath. At last they are able to talk alone and find that both can speak of things that they have kept secret before. May Day misunderstandings, when Dr Harrison is accused of being betrothed to two other ladies, rupture this happiness. Overcome by this public humiliation and perceived betrayal, Sophy collapses and is sent to stay with an aunt, out of the reach of Dr Harrison. Even when she returns with typhoid fever, he is forbidden to see her and she almost dies from the treatment that Dr Morgan pursues. When Frank is finally called, he must risk her life to save it. The drugs he uses can be so deadly that the dose is crucial. He sits with her through the night while the crisis of her illness breaks and she regains consciousness, and he vows never to leave her side again.

Miss Matty attends the wedding of Sophy Hutton to Dr Harrison and sees Sophy wear the white muslin that was intended for her own wedding dress.

Miss Matty, coming to call on Sophy, takes the back path through the orchard, so familiar from her girlhood. She is carrying a parcel wrapped in hessian and she pauses as she reaches the familiar cherry tree, and presses the parcel closer to her. She remembers so clearly her happiness the day that cherry tree was planted and how she had imagined all her future laid out before her. In the bedroom, which was once her own, she gives Sophy the parcel and asks if she will wear it for her wedding to Dr Harrison. It is the white muslin that her brother Peter had promised to send her for her own wedding dress when she married Mr Holbrook. 'It was meant for a Rectory bride, my dear, and now a Rectory bride will wear it.'

⋄❧ The Buxtons ❧⋄

O
N THE SUBJECT of gentlemen, the ladies of Cranford have no shortage of opinions, in spite of the distinct shortage of gentlemen in Cranford on which to base them. Peter Jenkyns and Captain Brown are two of the few men deemed to be agreeable, gentlemanly, and resourceful enough to satisfy their exacting standards; a third is Cranford native James Buxton.

The Buxton family had been respectable farmers who ploughed their own fields for several generations. Then, when James's grandfather discovered a seam of salt on his land, a hugely profitable mine was built to extract it. Believing that he should do something with his new-found wealth, James's grandfather abandoned their old farmhouse and built a mansion on the outskirts of Cranford, but immediately felt 'rather ashamed of what he had done; it seemed like stepping out of his position'. He and his wife never furnished the drawing rooms, feeling more at home sitting in the kitchen.

When James's father succeeded him, he and his wife gradually furnished the house and occupied it more fully, though they, too, were modest farmers at heart. 'They might, if ambitious, have taken their place as country gentry', but they were content with the simple pleasures of life, and decided to forgo giving their son an elite education at a boarding school, sending him instead for lessons with a taciturn local parson. This down-to-earth approach suited young James, who was 'singularly void of worldliness or ambition for himself' and was happiest when surrounded by family and friends. These friends included Peter and Matty Jenkyns, whom he had known since childhood. Though blunt-speaking and occasionally volatile, James has a generous heart and, like Peter, is fond of jokes, most of which are well known to his audience, 'for he worked a merry idea threadbare before he would let it go'.

He was considered a fine catch in his youth and so the young ladies of Cranford had to brook some disappointment when he chose for his bride

'It seemed probable that Mr Buxton, who was singularly void of worldliness or ambition for himself, would become worldly and ambitious for his son.'

Delighted to hear of his return to Cranford, Miss Matty calls on her childhood friend James Buxton.

a silversmith's daughter from Wrexham. Still, it was felt that he did the right thing by bringing her to live in Cranford, where they had a son, William, and later became guardians of Erminia, Mrs Buxton's orphaned goddaughter, a beautiful, wilful and warm-hearted girl.

And so the years passed in domestic tranquillity, with Mrs Buxton managing her husband's whims so adroitly that he hardly knew that she was the gentle ruler of the house. A cultivated woman herself, she took the house in hand, adding many of the finer touches and giving it, at last, a lived-in elegance. It was also her wish that William be well educated and Mr Buxton readily concurred, for his hopes for his son 'were all for honour and distinction'. William is sent to Eton and then Cambridge, but, during his first year, Mrs Buxton's health begins to fail and the family's contented life goes topsy-turvy. In the hope that warmer coastal air might effect a cure, Mr Buxton shutters up The Glebe and takes a house in Broadstairs on the south coast. There they pass two years before Mrs Buxton falls into a terminal decline. William abandons his studies altogether, and father and son keep a vigil by her side until her untimely death.

Return of the Native

Raw with grief, Mr Buxton looks forward to returning home to Cranford and so William sets off ahead of him to open up the house. Despite the shared loss, their grief manifests itself in contrary ways. Without Mrs Buxton's soothing influence to broker their relationship, Mr Buxton's hot temper has no control and William drifts with no clear goal in mind. They rub each other up the wrong way and are both inclined to mope.

When Matty and Mr Buxton resume their friendship, he is grateful for her offer to introduce William and Erminia to Edward and Peggy Bell, hopeful that the prospect of new local friendships might encourage William to stay in Cranford, for he longs to leave home – if he could but settle on the right career. William is excited by the advances of the age, and by engineering in particular. But when he suggests to his father that he might write to Mr Brunel himself and ask to be his apprentice, Mr Buxton is derisive. He is far more impressed with Edward Bell's plans to make money and a name for himself by practising law – so much so that, with ill-judged impulsiveness, he appoints the unqualified Edward as his land agent.

The cause of Mr Buxton's scorn has much to do with the course his own life had taken. He had been given the benefits of intelligence and wealth, but had capitalised on neither. He was indolent in his business affairs, and even boasted of this negligence, preferring to believe that no one would take advantage of him. But now, feeling guilty about his own laxity and wasted opportunities, he forms a plan for the future of his son, whom he fears is in danger of squandering his own assets. He determines that William should have a career of national significance, by representing Cranford in Parliament, and to achieve this decides that William will need to forge better social connections and 'marry up'.

That Mr Buxton had never discussed this ambition with his son might seem surprising; that it never occurred to him that William might oppose it is even more remarkable. But Mr Buxton's imperiousness comes from the fact that he has lived fifty years and more without ever having someone counter his will, and so 'there had not seemed a wish which he had it not in his power to gratify as soon as formed'. William is the first to thwart him when he announces that he loves Peggy Bell and plans to marry her.

Erminia's life 'was a shattered mirror; every part dazzling and brilliant, but wanting the coherency and perfection of a whole'.

Frustrated by his father's conservative thinking, William longs to leave home and carve a place for himself in the new industrial age.

*Being as wilful as
each other, William
and Mr Buxton are
unable to negotiate
a truce.*

*As William recovers
at home from the
railway accident,
his commitment to
Peggy never wavers.*

*Peggy brings
William a sprig of
gorse as a symbol
of enduring love.*

Mr Buxton is in no mood to reason. He does not deny that Peggy is a lovely girl but she's not the wife William will need if he is to make his mark in the world. Mr Buxton forbids the engagement and they quarrel bitterly.

But William has the same seeds of imperiousness in him and is determined he will not be treated like a child. Erminia advises that, if he wants to be regarded as an equal by his father, then he must *earn* his respect. Spurred by events and her words, William is at last focused and knows what he wants: to marry Peggy Bell and to become an engineer. He leaves home immediately and secures a lowly apprenticeship at the Railway Works with Captain Brown. It is a rude shock to go from living as comfortably as one pleased to the bleakness of toiling long hours with little reward in the bitter cold and wet of that long winter, with only a tent to call home. His sole consolation is in writing to Peggy and receiving her letters.

Mr Buxton blames Matty for his woes; if she had not interfered and introduced the two families, none of this would have happened. She is shocked by his reaction to the engagement but most hurt by his anger towards her. Having witnessed her own family torn apart after a falling out between father and son, the accusation that she's caused a similar fraction between Mr Buxton and William is deeply distressing.

Mr Buxton becomes unbearably isolated at home, but he remains as stubborn and determined as ever to win this battle. When it is revealed that Edward has embezzled his money, he sees his opportunity. He offers Peggy a bargain: if she will abandon any thought of marrying his son, he will help Edward to escape prosecution. Peggy refuses to give up William but her argument that Edward deserves a second chance strikes a chord; Mr Buxton acknowledges that he gave him too much responsibility and 'supervised him idly', so he agrees to finance a new start for Edward in Canada. Peggy's courage and determination to do what is right and accompany Edward impress Mr Buxton. But, even as he re-evaluates his opinion of Peggy, he still hopes that her long absence will weaken William's attachment to her, and he will have his way at last.

It takes the death of Edward and the grave injuries to William in the railway crash for Mr Buxton to comprehend how his anger and intransigence were party to tragedy. Humbled and ridden with guilt, he nurses his son with the same tender attention that he once gave his wife, and is rewarded with far more than he believes he deserves – a forgiving son who will flourish and marry for love, just as Mr Buxton did before him.

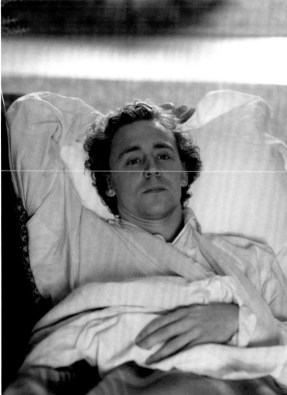

❧ The Bells ☙

ONE OF THE MORE curious sights in Cranford (a town not lacking in curiosities) is that of the widow Mrs Bell, wearing the blackest of widow's weeds, prostrating herself over her husband's grave each Sunday, while her children Peggy and Edward stand by, 'sensitively conscious how often they are pointed out' by passers-by. Mrs Bell is not unaware of her audience; indeed, her performance has become such a talking point in the town that she has come to feel it 'her duty' to maintain it indefinitely.

Once this weekly ritual at the graveside is concluded, the Bells walk home – turning out of the church lychgate and then following the field path for a mile or so until it reaches a common 'richly coloured with the golden gorse and the purple heather, which in summertime send out their warm scents into the quiet air'. Thorn Cottage sits a half-mile further on, in a sheltered basin surrounded by grassy hills. It is a very pleasant walk to and from church and that is just as well, for it constitutes the family's only excursion into society. 'They were as secluded in their green hollow as the households in the German forest-tales.'

This forlorn seclusion was due partly to Mrs Bell's acute sense of social inferiority, and partly to the unfortunate timing of their arrival into Cranford. No sooner had the ailing Mr Bell taken up his curacy under Reverend Hutton than his health declined and he died within the month. Mrs Bell went into mourning and withdrew the family from the small society that they had barely begun to know. As a year came and went, she found that coming out of mourning was far more difficult than going into it, and continued to decline invitations, thereby ensuring that she, Peggy and Edward remained isolated from everyone.

With little money to live on, Mrs Bell prides herself on running the house with 'decent frugality'. A small provision had been made in her husband's Will for the education of Edward, whose future was of great concern to both father and mother, while Peggy, being only a girl, is overlooked. And so, while Edward sits in 'the little book-room "studying" as he chose to call it' from a correspondence course, Peggy spends her day doing the housework and attending to Edward's many whims. Her

Mrs Bell 'was regularly asked by some one to stay to dinner after morning church, and as regularly declined, for she thought it her duty to go and cry over her husband's grave'.

Thorn Cottage, the secluded home of the Bell family.

Hoping that friendship between the younger Buxtons and Bells would benefit both families, Matty and Miss Pole try to convince the reclusive Mrs Bell to attend a luncheon at Mr Buxton's house.

mother relies heavily on her daughter, but holds no affection for her. She lives entirely for her domineering son, of whom she is rather afraid.

Peggy bears her situation in the household with considerable grace because of her gentle and loving nature. But as 'no one cared to hear what she had to say' at home, and with no social connections beyond it, she lives increasingly in her head, day-dreaming as she goes about her daily chores unnoticed.

Her favourite place is the spring, where she must go several times a day to fetch water. Hidden from the cottage down a steep slope, Peggy treasures it as her own private sanctuary. Gorse bushes line either side of the spring's bank, and over the grey rocks 'yellow stone-crop and scarlet-leaved crane's-bill grew luxuriantly'. It is here that she comes to dream 'in any scarce half-hour of leisure'; here, too, where she disappears to cry at her 'mother's sharp fault-finding', or take refuge 'when bidden to keep out of the way'.

New Friends and Horizons

It is around this time that Miss Matty begins to take an interest in Peggy, whom she observes is coming of age without a care being given for her future life or happiness. And so she resolves to widen Peggy's horizon by encouraging a friendship with the young people at the Buxton house.

At first, Edward is the keener of the two, as he is determined to make a name for himself in business and sees potential advantages to himself through contact with Mr Buxton. His clever talk impresses Mr Buxton, but William and Erminia are put off by his air of self-importance. Peggy they first think of as timid (when alone, they call her 'little mousey') but it soon becomes clear to Erminia that, with encouragement, Peggy will reveal the imaginative and spirited young woman that she truly is. She finds Peggy's candid and unaffected conversation refreshing (for, having had no training or experience in the finer points of social etiquette, Peggy simply says what she feels). Erminia soon finds Peggy indispensable, and William is often dispatched with an extra horse to collect her for visits. He, too, is surprised and delighted to find on these rides that Peggy is far from being the 'mousey' girl he first imagined.

By and by, Peggy begins to blossom under Matty's nurturing influence and the Buxton family's friendship. The young woman who at first disliked being noticed (feeling her outdated brown dress only made her stand out) now delights in wearing the pretty gowns passed on by Mary Smith. She is even more delighted when William happens to notice how lovely she looks in them. Her attraction to William comes upon her slowly, but, when he declares his love for her, 'the suddenness of her own heart' is unequivocal. Peggy is overjoyed, though she dreads telling her mother of her profound happiness because 'it seemed as yet so cobweb-like, as if a touch would spoil its beauty'.

This happiness is most certainly tested by events. Peggy's mother confesses herself astonished that William has fallen for a girl with 'no charm' and Mr Buxton violently opposes the engagement. Despite her disappointment, Peggy refrains from anger, understanding that Mr Buxton has acted out of love for his son, though she still determines to stand fast with William. And it is this natural compassion and calm resolve which steadies both herself and William during their most trying of times.

Edward profits greatly from the falling out of Mr Buxton and William. Fuelled by disappointment and anger at his son, Mr Buxton agrees to

finance Edward's law studies in Manchester and employs him to handle the sale of his cottages at Tinden Edge to the railway company. This is Edward's chance to impress and he is ruthless in his dealings with the tenants, serving immediate eviction notices on them. He cares nothing for the plight of Bella Gregson, who will have five homeless children, for 'worldly success was his standard of merit. The end seemed with him to justify the means.' But Edward too is vulnerable. He is unused to handling such large sums of money and gives in to temptation, using some of it on drink and the gaming tables of Manchester. He is soon so deeply in debt that he knows, if caught, he will be charged with fraud and embezzlement, a crime that carries the possibility of transportation to Australia. He runs home and begs Peggy to help him escape.

Edward is drawn into a life of dissolution in Manchester, and he embezzles Mr Buxton's money to finance it.

Peggy blossoms under the nurturing influence of William and his family.

A Test of Character

Peggy is sickened by Edward's crimes but is just as shocked by Mr Buxton's attempt to blackmail her into giving up William, by offering to help her brother if she does. Her courage, loyalty and love are then questioned by her mother and Edward, who both assume that she will be prepared to make this sacrifice. They see it as nothing less than her duty.

This family crisis resonates deeply with her loyal friend Miss Matty. Having been in a comparable position years before when she gave up Mr Holbrook to protect her own family's happiness, she knows how much this sacrifice would cost her young friend. Matty refrains from advising Peggy what to do, but her influence is felt. For Peggy, steered by her own moral compass, and with a new-found strength through the loving friendships of Matty, William and Erminia, finds the courage to say in her 'simple and utterly truthful' manner that she will not give up William. And, in urging Mr Buxton to help Edward regardless, she follows the only path where she will betray neither her heart nor her brother.

She will be sorely tested by events, but Peggy never wavers from her determination to do what she feels to be right. She comes to accept that she will never secure the longed-for affection of her mother, but is rewarded when Mr Buxton finally sanctions her engagement to William – with a life of her own, full of love, respect and happiness. And Miss Matty, too, seeing Peggy and William united in love, finds a reward of a very personal kind.

Miss Pole's Advices to a Lady Living Abroad

MISS POLE HAS always been an enthusiastic correspondent, penning many a letter to keep her acquaintances *'au fait* as to the proceedings of the dear little town'. In her letters to Mary Smith, she matches every sentence of news with an instruction for some new commission that can only be achieved in Manchester; cheaper crochet wool, perhaps, or cuttlefish to keep her parrot's beak in trim. But since Miss Jessie Brown married Major Gordon and took up residence in India more than a year since, a particularly lively and regular correspondence has developed between them. By this means Miss Pole not only keeps Jessie up to date with proceedings in the household of her father and her new step-mamma, but is most fortunately able to pass on her wisdom and knowledge of life on that distant continent.

Miss Pole seals her letter to Jessie Brown, which contains news of the town, titbits from the local paper and much advice.

28 January 1845

My dear Jessie,

How splendid it is, to hear News of your safe delivery of a Daughter! Although we all shook our heads at the thought of you in India; it cannot have been convenient, being brought to Bed so far from Johnson's Stores. When dear Caroline was confined, Miss Tomkinson was at the counter daily, in perpetual pursuit of Fuller's Earth, and Pins, and Dr Phalp's Tincture For Relief of Headache. (Though it was not the new Mamma who suffered from this ailment, it rather being for Miss Tomkinson's own use. She was charged with the butcher's Twins for the full fortnight's lying in.)

The new babe is a most colossal Boy, was baptised Horace, and has Ginger curls much the colour of his father's. It is a very violent shade, which I fear speaks of the choleric Humour. Mrs Forrester opines that, in due course, Master Horace will make an immense match for your Girl, but Mrs Jamieson deems the notion quite repugnant. Little Flora is, after all, step-grandchild of a lady once married to a Baron, whilst Horace's Papa is a peddler of pork Fancies.

The former Lady Glenmire has settled well in Cranford. Your father chose well when he took her for his Wife, for she embodies every virtue most cherished in our Town. She is a scrupulous Hostess, who does not shirk her turn in the round of Entertainment. Her Refreshments are not vulgar; her meringues being served quite innocent of Cream (which would only occasion a deal of grease and smearing) and in short 'elegant economy' has become her Watchword. This very week she cut up her tam-o'-shanter and shaped it instead into a charming Reticule; it is a most ingenious contrivance, with a pocket for her playing cards, and she still has her feathered Straw for church on Sundays. Meanwhile her skill upon the piano forte is very much admired, though we were rendered somewhat warm by the ballad 'No! John! No!' (Not all the Ladies were persuaded that this was the story of a bad Dog jumping Up.)

When we gathered for Whist, to celebrate your Child's arrival, our Conversation turned to the subject of your wardrobe, in particular the yellow Silk you wore to go Away. Even in our temperate land, sunshine is a most corrupting Force, apt to bleed all brightness from the colour of a Gown, and silk is especially vulnerable to fading. REMEMBER! A despoiled garment can be unpicked, and then sewn back with all the pieces faced the other way. This method can be repeated (though the enlivening Effect is apt to be diminished) and I well recall a Pea Green frock of dear Miss Deborah's, which was turned twice, and became – sequentially – a Window blind, a peg Bag, and a trivet Mat, before its days were considered to be done.

As you will of course recall, in Cheshire silk clothing is preserved for Best, and laid away with Tonka beans, calculated to repulse the Moth. Nothing sullies the Toilette so much as garments which are spotted, stained, or gnawed upon by these rapacious beasts, and every Lady of rectitude keeps six or seven Brooches in supply, to be pinned over flaws in costume. Pewter, filigree and shell are all popular in Cranford, though I myself have an Agate butterfly, which sits so well on the darn in my Damask that one might imagine it alive.

On the Topic of dress, Mr Peter Jenkyns tells us that in India, Infants are swaddled in brocade and fed on jellied monkey meat! Dear Miss Matty is made quite distraught by this. Her supervision of little Tilly Hearne has made her a mistress of juvenile hygiene, and she urges Cambric upon an infant's skin, with bread and milk thrice daily and a spoonful of treacle to pique appetite (if listless). She was greatly exercised last Michaelmas, when Tilly looked likely to run about too soon. Matron Slingsby, in her volume on the Maternal Management Of Children, predicts bow-legs when ambulation starts before the eighteenth month is out. Seeking to contain the child, Miss Matty followed the Matron's advice, which is to put both legs into one long Stocking.

I was pleased to knit this corrective Garment, in purl stitch, and it proved so efficacious that I have fashioned a second, for dear Flora. I will send it on, with the Blackcurrant wine Mrs Forrester has kept for you, as soon as she acquires a leather bottle for the Post.

(NOTA BENE: It has to be remarked that the burning of the Haberdasher's shop at Newton is a Boon. All the wool there smells of Smoke, and is being sold off at three ha'pence for the Ball. At that price, the odour can be easily ignored, and if one is clever with one's Needles it all comes up the same when knitted.)

My candle sputters as I write; Mr Johnson says that when the railway line is finished, there will be Gas lamps in this Street. I suppose that once this comes to pass, we can dispense with Candles altogether in the evening, as long as we leave our curtains parted wide. Though Jem Hearne will not be able to stand in the shadows and court Mr Buxton's housemaid Margaret, as I have seen him doing these two Sunday evenings past.

I am glad you cannot hear the navvies as they swagger by my house. They sing all the way to the George, in uncouth Irish voices, and last week made a Convenience of my fence. I went to Johnson's for chloride of lime, only to find they had increased its price. I called Mrs Johnson a railway Profiteer, which judgement she accepted without rancour, and something altogether like a Smile.

She will not be Smiling when we climb on the Train in King Street, and travel to Manchester to do our shopping there.

Yours, as ever,
Octavia Pole (Miss)

As dictated to Miss Heidi Thomas
(Miss Pole's finger being in a Bandage on
account of the misbehaviour of her parrot)

Capturing the Moment

⊰ Filming ⊱

F ILM-MAKING is just problem solving: how best to tell the story in the screenplay; how to realise the demands of the script; how to pull off the technical feats required; how to finance it all. The skill lies in bringing together the most creative and technically talented cast and crew to form the company that will solve these problems together, a task that fell to the Producer and Co-producer.

Sue was the Producer, a job that is a mystery to most people outside the world of filming, and equally opaque to many within it, because the role differs according to the project. Some producers come up through the technical route, starting on the floor as runner, then assistant director, moving to production manager. This is the route that Co-producer Rupert Ryle-Hodges took and it has given him an invaluable knowledge of all technical and financial aspects of production. Some, like Sue, come through the route of acting, writing and directing. With their complementary skills, they chose the personnel – Rupert engaging the production team, film crew, facilities and catering teams, and Sue selecting the creative heads of department, with whom she would work in both the planning and the realisation of the entire production through all its many stages until it was on screen. Some heads of department, like Susie, were already on board: she was the Script Executive, working closely with Heidi Thomas on the development of the scripts, and overseeing rewrites throughout filming. Others joined the team when the programme was green-lit and pre-production began in earnest.

In this chapter we've selected a few parts out of the many months of production and filming over both series, and hope – by detailing how these sections were tackled – to shed some light on the whole process. It is not a chronological account from script to screen, but rather a selection of scenes – some large scale, some merely fragments – to illustrate how the different departments worked together to create *Cranford*.

We'll let the cast and the heads of departments speak for themselves as much as possible. Everyone involved in the production is listed in the next chapter but, to help navigate this one, here are the names and jobs of those quoted or referred to.

Director: Simon Curtis

Writer: Heidi Thomas

Producer: Sue Birtwistle

Script Executive: Susie Conklin

Co-producer: Rupert Ryle-Hodges

Casting Director: Maggie Lunn

Director of Photography: Ben Smithard

Production Designer: Donal Woods

Costume Designer: Jenny Beavan

Make-up & Hair Designers: Alison Elliott & Karen Hartley-Thomas

Sound Recordist: Peter Brill

Sound Mixer: Paul Hamblin

Choreography &

Etiquette: Jane Gibson

Location Manager: Richard May

Film Editor: Phil Booth

Film Editor: Fran Parker

Composer: Carl Davis

[*Cast photographs on pp.148–9*]

The camera team tracks along with Judi Dench and Lisa Dillon in the May Day scene where they discuss Miss Matty's bankruptcy.

❧ Lacock into Cranford ❧

THE SEARCH TO FIND our Cranford began in January 2004. January is never the best time to go on the road to hunt for locations; the days are short and the light so grey that nowhere looks at its best. The driving to and from potential locations is done in the dark, so that no daylight is wasted.

We had been given development money from BBC Drama Productions to put together an informed budget before any commitment could be made to move into production. One of the main costs of such a drama is when the Unit has to film away from the London base, so the brief is always to try to shoot as much as possible close to London, to save on travel and hotel costs. But with a story set in a small rural market town in the 1840s, some locations would be impossible to find in London (or indeed anywhere) and the town of Cranford was one of them. It was clear we would have to search further afield, but still as close to London as possible, with fast road and rail links to the capital.

Gerry Scott had worked with Susie and me as Production Designer on both *Pride and Prejudice* and *Wives and Daughters* so I asked her to help find our Cranford. We had both filmed twice in Lacock and Gerry felt we should try to find a different place to put on screen so, over the next few weeks, we searched through Kent, Hampshire, Wiltshire, Somerset, Gloucestershire, Oxfordshire, Hertfordshire and Staffordshire.

We had, of course, already considered Knutsford, the town about which Gaskell had written *Cranford*. But twenty-first-century Knutsford is a successful and busy modern town, and the work needed to hide this modern success, combined with its distance from London, made it too expensive to contemplate.

Lacock

In the end, we accepted that there are very good reasons why people choose to film in Lacock. It is a Wiltshire village owned almost entirely by the National Trust and all the buildings are listed, so there have been strict limits on what has been done to the properties. This means that there

The Grip pushes the camera dolly to keep pace with the actors walking briskly down the other side of King Street.

Turning the Red Lion pub into Johnson's Universal Stores was the biggest task facing the design and construction teams in Lacock.

would be comparatively little 'negative work' to be done by the design team, before they could fashion it into Cranford. There are no television aerials, no overhead power lines, no parking meters, no traffic lights – all the things that would have to be removed, either literally or by disguising them, before filming. But for Production Designer Donal Woods, who took over from Gerry when pre-production finally started in 2007, the most appealing aspect is the mixed architecture, which chimes exactly with Gaskell's description of Cranford.

The National Trust welcomes filming because it helps to generate income for the upkeep of its properties; income not only from the film company, but also from the increase in paying visitors afterwards. But Lacock is a living, working village and it is vital that the community is consulted before a decision is made, because filming is very disruptive. A comprehensive proposal is drawn up, detailing everything that we would want to do whilst there: the construction work required before filming; which parts of the town would be used and when; car parking arrangements; and a hundred other things that would be needed to keep the village functioning as near as possible to normal.

Richard May: 'Because Lacock has had film crews before, they know what to expect. Generally, they find it interesting and support the idea but, at the same time, no one wants their lives to be disrupted. People need to get to work on time, take their children to the school, keep their businesses open, and have somewhere to park their car. An evening meeting in the village hall is set up to which everyone is invited and the hall is crowded. Sue, Rupert and I explain the proposal in detail and everyone has a chance to ask questions. At the end of the evening, a vote is taken on whether the village will accept the filming. It's a very nerve-racking moment! Fortunately, the vote was almost unanimously in favour.'

Design

Donal Woods: 'The first thing to do is to pick the right buildings in the village to suit our characters. The Red Lion pub in Lacock is a prominent building on the main street, so that's chosen to be Johnson's Universal Stores, on what we would call King Street. We would build a ground-floor façade over the whole front of the pub that would contain the

ever-changing window displays of the store. This would be our biggest construction job and the team would move in ten days ahead of the Unit to build that and the Lock-up.'

Dr Harrison and Miss Galindo will both live on King Street, so the most likely exteriors have to be chosen for them. On the smaller street (our Princess Street), Miss Deborah and Miss Matty Jenkyns will live, directly opposite which there must be a suitably small house for Captain Brown. The script requires Miss Pole's tiny house to have a garden; as none on this street does, a house that is set slightly back from the others is chosen and the design team build an instant garden, complete with railings, path and gate. Apart from the odd glimpse into a hall, none of the interiors of the houses will be filmed here; all will be built on the sound stages back in London, giving much more flexibility to both how the scenes can be shot and how they can be scheduled. So, meticulous measurements must be taken on location to ensure that there is no discrepancy from interior to exterior shot.

The transforming moment: once the cars are removed and the ground cover laid, Lacock becomes Cranford.

The camera operator, Roger Pearce, needs the Grip's steadying hand as he shoulders the weight of the camera to film on the move. Adam Coles keeps the shot in focus.

Apart from that, all that is needed in both streets is small changes to door furniture, window dressings for shops, curtains hanging at windows to hide modern décor inside, and the downpipes to be painted in a period colour. Horse troughs and hitching posts for the horses are added. Finally, all the residents' cars are moved to their new parking field and seventy tons of ground cover is laid over the entire area, which for the next week will be our set. This is the transforming moment, when twenty-first-century Lacock becomes Cranford of the 1840s. Most people agree that, with all the modern disparate elements removed, the scale and beauty of the village is revealed. Director Simon Curtis: 'It feels like the most extraordinary studio lot in history. You really do feel transported back in time.'

Restrictions

The most valuable commodity in Lacock is the hospitality and welcome of the people. One could easily borrow Jessie Brown's comment on Cranford: 'What a place for kindness Lacock is!' It must at times be very difficult to be asked to stay in your house for an extra ten minutes or wait to pop into the shop while a shot is finished. Without their goodwill the enterprise would be impossible.

There are, of course, certain restrictions that are agreed up-front: we will only film in two of the streets, and never at the same time; one street must always be open for access. This of course makes the scheduling tougher because if, say, the camera is following characters from one place in the town to another, that sequence will have to be shot on two separate occasions, possibly days apart. This will mean that the costume, hair and make-up will have to be repeated.

Night filming there is also difficult, especially as we try to shoot when the days are longest. Normally a night shoot could continue into the early hours but, with our set being the streets where people hope to sleep, we had to finish our few night shoots at 11 pm to ensure everything was clear and quiet by midnight. Night scenes can be very potent for storytelling but, when it doesn't get dark enough till after 9.30 pm, this makes for a very short shooting time. So we had to address this in the script and find ways to shift night exterior scenes to other places, or to find other solutions to the problem (as in Darkness Lane, pp.214–15).

Snow

During the scripting stage of the second series, we were pleased to discover that the winter of 1844 had been particularly harsh, because this would mirror the bleakness that envelops the town following the decision to allow the railway to enter. Families quarrel, old friendships splinter, the young start to leave; the warmth seems to be disappearing from Cranford and by mid-November, when the train is derailed with such dire consequences, snow is already starting to fall, heralding bitter times ahead. The first series had ended with a wedding, something we did not want to repeat.

We talked at length about the possibility of ending with a white Christmas; would it be too much of a cliché? We certainly wanted to finish with something uplifting as, in story terms, the town goes through so much to embrace change and re-establish harmony. And we longed to see the whole of King Street on Christmas Eve covered in snow with our Amazons walking down it together. Of course, it wasn't as easy as that.

The night shoot: the A' camera on top of the crane with the 'B' camera below it simultaneously film the ladies walking through the snow.

Everyone agreed that if we were going to do it, then it had to look convincing, and snow on film is costly. There are many different ways of representing snow on screen, so detailed discussions followed with all departments: Did we want 'a light covering here and there', or 'thick snow from near to far'? Would the ladies walk through the snow in shot? Did the roofs of all the houses have to be covered? And, most importantly, was the snow still to be falling as they walked? Each option has a different price tag and a different length of time attached to bring it about.

We finally opted for a combination of solutions: there would be a lighter (cheaper) version of the snow made from finely milled wood pulp in the background; from the Lock-up forward to the camera would be thicker snow, made from recycled paper, which would be more realistic for the ladies to walk on. The porches would have a light snow pumped on to them; the roofs would be given an icy sheen in CGI (computer-generated imaging) in post-production. Snow would be falling during the scene, but would be supplemented later in the close-ups by the visual effects team.

Ben Smithard judges that the light is right to start the night shoot. Simon Curtis prays for the snow to stay 'deep and crisp and even'.

Once the decision had been made that creatively it was right to aim for this ambitious scene, everything needed to be planned in meticulous detail. A technical recce was set up and everyone who was to be involved

met at the location to discuss all the possibilities. Phil Booth laid out the given boundaries. Because of the light, we would not be able to start shooting until 9.30 pm. If we could guarantee a quicker than usual get-out at the end, we would perhaps have two hours to film the whole scene, which involved four of our leading ladies, a child actor and a cow. The ladies would have to walk the length of King Street wearing long dresses with cloaks and hoods and, strapped on their boots would be metal pattens – a sort of 1840s version of the mountain-climbing crampon. And after every take, they would have to move back into place and fresh snow would need to be re-sprayed to cover the footprints.

To achieve this, Phil was clear that everything had to be rehearsed ahead of time. The actresses would need to be in costume and make-up, the whole crew in place and ready to shoot as soon as Ben Smithard felt

the light was right. There would be two enormous cranes in the street: one at the top end hidden behind the houses would provide back lighting; the bigger one at the other end would carry the 'A' camera, operated by Ben. This crane would start with a very high shot of the whole snowy street and, as the Amazons walked down the street towards it, it would dip lower and move closer to them, to end on a tighter shot of the four ladies. The 'B' camera, operated by Hamish Doyne-Ditmas, would be on the ground to get individual close-ups.

The snow would take at least two hours to lay over the entire street. While all this was being set up, the Unit moved to Miss Pole's house to shoot two small exterior scenes. Briefly, it rained heavily which delayed not only the scenes, but also the laying of the snow. Water dissolves the paper-based snow. We stood around under plastic tents and umbrellas until it stopped. The sun came out and the scenes were nearly completed when Sue was asked to go and see the finished snow. Turning the corner, a magical sight: the place had been transformed into a winter wonderland! Everything that had been hoped for was now set. Supper break was called and everyone went back to base, tensed ready for the night shoot ahead, but excited. And then it started to rain.

It rained very heavily for half an hour and washed all the snow away. Seeing it happen really was watching money go down the drain, as the snow dissolved and disappeared. Decisions had to be made quickly. If it stopped raining, would the road dry quickly enough to take the snow again? Would we have time to re-lay the snow and still shoot the scene? Could we afford to do it? Should we instead resolve to go without any snow? Sue and Rupert knew that cuts would have to be made later on to compensate but, as the rain stopped, the spirit of the team was to try to achieve the scene as planned, so the go-ahead was given to re-lay the snow.

Everyone worked fast together to get the whole scene re-set and amazingly we started shooting on time. It seemed the whole town wanted to watch this event take place. In every bedroom along King Street, a party gathered with glasses of wine. We had asked that no lights be switched on and no flash photographs taken and, miraculously, everyone cooperated. Local television had announced our plans and hundreds of spectators turned up unexpectedly. Barriers were erected behind the crane and the good-natured crowd complied with our request to keep silent during the takes.

Wrap was called at a quarter to midnight, fifteen minutes later than planned but the whole town had joined in the spirit of the scene, almost as if it really was Christmas in Cranford. The following day, within four hours, the ground cover was removed, the street cleaned and the residents moved their cars back. No sign of the filming remained.

Christmas Eve: the Amazons walk through the crisp snow to the party at the Assembly Rooms.

Imelda Staunton: 'I really did feel as if I was in a Christmas card. It was so beautiful it took my breath away. I wanted to stay all night. But of course you have to get on with the job; you can't be skipping around saying: "Oh, I love it here!" But it felt very special.'

Judi Dench: 'It was wonderful because it really was like walking on freshly fallen snow. And it was summer, so it was quite remarkable, because if you've got a covering of snow, you actually start to feel quite cold.'

✧ Casting ✧

ASTING A PRODUCTION on the scale of *Cranford* was a joyful challenge. Most dramas revolve around maybe half a dozen characters but, because so many stories had been interwoven here, it called for a cast of over forty actors, the majority of whom would need to be leading players. It is very unusual to have so many featured roles in one piece, and even more unusual to require principal actors sometimes to be present at the edges of other people's scenes. But it is in the nature of *Cranford* that everyone's stories connect and are of consequence to others. We realised that what we needed was the equivalent of a theatre company. We started at the heart of the piece by finding the Amazons, the leading actresses who made up the core of our drama and would become the centre of our company.

Maggie Lunn: '*Cranford* was always seen as an ensemble piece, so it was important to get the chemistry of this group right. We had to keep an eye out for the different shapes and sizes, but it's mainly the character and warmth of the actresses that matters. Sue had already asked Judi to play Miss Matty and that obviously helps because everyone in the universe wants to work with her.'

In fact, all the actresses cast as Amazons had been on the Dream Cast List from well before we had finished the storylines. Eileen Atkins was always our first choice for Miss Deborah and we had all pictured Imelda as Miss Pole when plotting her scenes. Deborah Findlay and Barbara Flynn, who had been in the production we did of Gaskell's *Wives and Daughters*, were already on the list and, as Julia McKenzie remembers: 'In 2001, I was doing a play with Judi in the West End and afterwards, at the first-night party, Sue took me into a corner and said: "I have the most wonderful part for you." I said I'd like to read the script but it turned out it was still just ideas on cards! But it did happen in the end and I did get the wonderful part.'

Julia Sawalha, Barbara Flynn, Julia McKenzie and Lesley Manville unpack their offerings for the Amazons' Bake-a-cake day.

The principal actors in Cranford. (Overleaf)

Eileen Atkins
Miss Deborah Jenkyns

Judi Dench
Miss Matty Jenkyns

Nicholas Le Prevost
Mr Peter Jenkyns

Lisa Dillon
Mary Smith

Andrew Buchan
Jem Hearne

Claudie Blakley
Martha

Finty Williams
Clara Smith

Barbara Flynn
The Hon. Mrs Jamieson

Imelda Staunton
Miss Pole

Julia McKenzie
Mrs Forrester

Deborah Findlay
Miss Tomkinson

Selina Griffiths
Caroline Tomkinson

Celia Imrie
Lady Glenmire

Jim Carter
Captain Brown

Julia Sawalha
Jessie Brown

Alistair Petrie
Major Gordon

Simon Woods
Dr Harrison

Joe McFadden
Dr Marshland

John Bowe
Dr Morgan

Lesley Manville
Mrs Rose

Francesca Annis
Lady Ludlow

Rory Kinnear
Septimus Hanbury

Greg Wise
Sir Charles Maulver

Emma Fielding
Miss Galindo

Philip Glenister
Mr Carter

Alex Etel
Harry Gregson

Emma Lowndes
Bella Gregson

Dean Lennox Kelly
Job Gregson

Alex Jennings
Reverend Hutton

Kimberley Nixon
Sophy Hutton

Adrian Scarborough
Mr Johnson

Debra Gillett
Mrs Johnson

Jonathan Pryce
Mr Buxton

Tom Hiddleston
William Buxton

Michelle Dockery
Erminia Whyte

Michael Gambon
Mr Holbrook

Lesley Sharp
Mrs Bell

Jodie Whittaker
Peggy Bell

Matthew McNulty
Edward Bell

Tim Curry
Signor Brunoni

☙ Finding the Character ❧

T HERE IS NO one right method to approach the playing of a role. All actors have to find their own particular way into a character and they normally keep secret the alchemy they practise to create this new being. But it's likely that the process begins with the script – both in what your character says and what is said about you – but it might also evolve in production in early discussions with the director and producer, or later in rehearsals with the other cast. Some actors find the initial sessions with the costume and make-up designers help them discover the key to the part; some are helped immeasurably by the sets, props and the locations.

Miss Pole

Imelda Staunton: 'When I was first offered the part of Miss Pole, I didn't want to do it because I thought: "I don't want her to be just a busybody." Then I read the script again and wondered: "What if she was really a very serious person who felt responsible for passing on vital information, that it was a genuine job for her to do?" And then I had a real hook on the part.'

Sir Charles Maulver

Greg Wise: 'There's something quite wonderful about wearing britches, big boots, waistcoats and cravats that really sets you in the world you are supposed to be inhabiting.'

Lady Ludlow

Francesca Annis: 'It was quite fun putting myself together as Lady Ludlow because she is completely different visually from me. I had this big high wig, all grey, which I called Marge, as in Marge in *The Simpsons*. When I put on grey Marge, I started to feel like Lady Ludlow. And when I took her off, I'd have a shriek and become myself again!'

Jenny Beavan: 'Lady Ludlow is a very interesting character in *Cranford* because she is steeped in the eighteenth century. Our ladies tend to be very 1830s in their dress, whereas Lady Ludlow is a mixture of eighteenth century and 1820s. When Francesca came for her fitting, she was very knowledgeable and full of amazing ideas for the detail of her costumes. It helped enormously and I think we all found Lady Ludlow together.

'Alison Elliott had worked out with Francesca that Lady Ludlow would have a very white pressed-powdered look to her face; very eighteenth century. She used to send the wig over for the costume fittings and it made such a difference, because Francesca looks so ridiculously young and beautiful. But the minute she put on this wig she became Lady Ludlow, and then we knew to go powdery with the colours of her frock.'

Francesca: 'It's not so much that I like the dressing up, but I love the idea of moving and existing in a very different time. Then the wonderful thing of being in the location, in costume, is that after a day or two I begin to feel like I own the place. I start to think: "This is really pleasant, this is mine."'

Greg Wise as Sir Charles Maulver and Francesca Annis as Lady Ludlow.

Miss Matty Jenkyns

Judi Dench: 'If you open a door and walk into rooms that look like the description in the book, it does the job for you. You feel that these are places that you know every corner of, that you really understand, that you actually live in. If you have to read a letter and care has gone into the handwriting and feel of the paper, it helps tremendously. When you get such skilful people doing the sets, the costumes, the make-up, the props, well, that's over half of my work done for me.'

Lisa Dillon and Judi Dench in the Jenkyns' parlour. Real elm beams, recovered from a demolished barn, were used to add authenticity to the studio set.

Miss Deborah Jenkyns

Eileen Atkins: 'At my costume fitting, I was given a large pair of flat boots to wear that stuck out a long way from under my dress. They were very masculine. I suddenly thought: "I know now what Deborah's like. I know how she walks."'

Lady Glenmire

Celia Imrie: 'At my costume fitting, Jenny had an old piece of tartan she had found which had marvellous moth holes in it. And that was perfect, as the ladies in the church describe her as not wearing a particularly all-it's-cracked-up-to-be gown. So the fact that this tartan is beaten up was just right. And we used it in quite a lot of scenes. It was Lady Glenmire's theme tune, if you like.

'If I tried on an old dress at the costume house Cosprop, and it didn't entirely work, Jenny would find a very old piece of material and have it copied; not to look brand new, which wouldn't have been right for Lady Glenmire, because she wasn't as rich as everybody imagined. I loved all that sort of detail, the fact that everything looks as if it's been worn and you've lived in it. The clothes never look like a costume. I also adored the fact that I got to wear a sort of tam-o'-shanter, which was a rather glorious contrast to all the famous bonnets!'

Jim Carter drives the gig, and Celia Imrie sports Lady Glenmire's old tartan and tam-o'-shanter.

❦ The Read-through ❧

ABOUT A WEEK before filming starts, a day is set aside for the scripts to be read aloud by the full cast in the presence of all who are involved in the production. This may be the only time we will all be together in the same place until the cast and crew screening, just before transmission. Although an intimidating event for the actors (and none, however experienced, is immune to this fear of having to represent their character before fully rehearsing), it is a vital step in the production. The words are meant to be heard, not read and, having listened to the entire scripts, we are able to make final story adjustments and dialogue polishes before we are caught up in the pressures of filming. It is important too because there are many distinct stages to a production and most people will be involved in only one of them, so may be unaware of the huge range of different skills that will be brought into play. By meeting each other, we can see how each of us fits into the whole piece.

Jenny Brassett, Production Co-ordinator: 'The read-through is the first impression that everyone gets of the production they are about to embark on and it's so important for everybody to feel they are going to be cared for. If a high standard is set at the very beginning, everyone feels in safe hands and steps up to the mark. The most amazing cast and crew had been assembled and that made me determined to make it the best read-through everyone had ever attended.

'Sue's brief was clear: We were on a tight budget, but she wanted the best. No plastic, no paper tablecloths and no polystyrene! The little money allowed would have to stretch far and be supplemented with creativity. So, white linen tablecloths and china cups, but only four bunches of daffodils artfully divided between small glasses round the horseshoe of tables set up in the beautiful Orangery at Shepperton Studios. The whole process was a team effort: a superb table plan from Camilla, the Assistant Co-ordinator, while Jon, Sue's Assistant, compiled the lists and sent out invitations. Trisha, our Set Decorator, begged Chinese screens and huge planters of greenery from the prop house. Rupert became convinced that I was organising a wedding!

'The read-through was to start at 10am and finish at 5pm – a whole day of catering for 120 on a tight budget. We almost had a disaster when I went to supervise the lunch presentation only to see that the sandwiches had been laid on the tables still in their plastic trays. "No plastic, no paper, no polystyrene!" Fortunately, we had time to get them on to china plates and no one knew what might have been. The final touch was planned like a military campaign: as soon as the read-through ended, Sue wanted everyone to have a glass of champagne in their hand within a minute. As we were only divided from the reading by the Chinese screens, this involved a lot of tiptoeing and the silent easing of corks.'

Celia Imrie: 'On the dot after the last sentence was read, Jenny and Jon led the whole team out with trays of champagne. I've never seen such a thing! If there'd been a fanfare playing I wouldn't have been surprised. Read-throughs are rather nerve-racking, but this was just wonderful.'

[Please note: The BBC has a strict policy of not buying champagne on productions or for parties. Any champagne mentioned in this book was purchased privately.]

Simon Woods (Dr Harrison) and Joe McFadden (Dr Marshland) still smiling as we reach the end of Episode Four.

∘❧ Etiquette ❧∘

T O FULLY inhabit a character from the 1840s, there's more for an actor to take on board than the patterns of speech or mode of dress particular to that time. If the etiquette of the period becomes second nature, it can provide insight into the physical and psychological behaviour of the character, as well as contributing to the truthfulness of the storytelling.

Jane Gibson: 'During rehearsals, I worked with as many actors as I could all together so they were interrelating, because a lot of etiquette from this period is to do with how men relate to women. For instance, when a woman comes into a room the man gets up and he waits for her to sit before he sits. Simple details, but things that are going out of our common memory. I try to communicate to the actors the meaning of these movements, because otherwise nobody really understands what they are doing or why. Movements of courtesy towards each other were used to oil social behaviour, and they also indicated status. Because Cranford's very hierarchical, everybody has a place and knows it. When two men meet, for example, there are rules about who should be seen to be bowing first. And the servants have a different way of making a curtsy from the middle and upper classes, because they are receiving orders and making a little bob and going off and doing it. So their curtsies come from a different place.

'I'm very keen that etiquette isn't seen as some airy-fairy thing, some generalised movements with no real meaning. These courtesies are all about making someone else feel comfortable and happy to be in your company. So you're not thinking about yourself, you're thinking about other people around you. And that's where good manners come from.'

Philip Glenister: 'If you're playing in a contemporary piece you can be much freer with your movements and perhaps ad lib a bit more, whereas in this period you are much more restricted in your actions and social graces. It's a good discipline for an actor to have because it makes you stand and walk in a certain way.'

◦⊱ The Operation ⊰◦

PERHAPS THE MOST intricate and enjoyable task during script development was the process of taking the separate storylines that originated in the three Gaskell novels and interweaving them to form a new whole – <u>our</u> *Cranford*. Each succession of rewrites brought new ideas about how best we could make one story impact on another; how seemingly unrelated characters could be influenced by each other. A vivid example of this process can be seen in the operation sequence.

Heidi Thomas: 'In *Mr Harrison's Confessions* there was this dramatic sequence with a local gardener who fell and broke his wrist. Sue and Susie had put the story in the first episode, which was a brilliant idea because it showed the whole community responding to the fact that one of their members had had this accident and the interaction of the classes was very good. And a medical story will always grab the audience's attention.'

As we worked on the early drafts of the scripts it became apparent that while the sequence was dramatic in itself, we needed to find ways to connect it with the ladies of the town – characters who came from the novel *Cranford*, and so weren't part of the original Dr Harrison story. Meanwhile, our commissioning executives at the BBC had asked us to look at cutting back on characters overall, as they felt it was confusing, and potentially too expensive, to have so many.

Heidi: 'At this point we started to look at amalgamating minor characters who had traits in common and found that because some had been based on the same real people originally, their characters could be combined. It seemed sensible to merge the gardener, who didn't have a story beyond the accident in the first episode, with the lovely character of Jem Hearne, who didn't have much to do in the early part of the series, but was going to play a significant role later when he falls in love with Martha.'

Not only did it up the dramatic stakes to have a younger man suffer a catastrophic injury that could disable him and send him to the workhouse, but his romantic connection with the Jenkyns' maid Martha gave an ideal opportunity to knit those stories more closely together.

The Fracture and Treatment

Heidi: 'There is very little detail given in the book about the injury or the revolutionary procedure Dr Harrison performed, and so Sue introduced me to the programme's medical consultant, Dr Martin Scurr, who is such a wonderfully learned man with a great passion for medical history. And I asked him what sort of arm injury would have necessitated an amputation at that time.'

Martin Scurr: 'We conceived that when Jem falls out of the tree, he puts his arm out to save himself and lands on his outstretched palm, and so the radius snaps and pokes through as all that weight comes down on top of it. Doctors at that time knew from experience that if a bone was coming through the skin the patient would get what they called putrefaction (what we would call gangrene today). The limb would die because of infection.

The scene of the accident: Jem Hearne climbs Miss Tomkinson's tree, but a branch can't bear his weight and he crashes to the ground.

But in the 1840s they had no concept of infection because Pasteur didn't elaborate his germ theory until 1865. So they had no idea about why the limb would rot and fall off and probably kill the patient with septicaemia. They used to believe it was because of what they called the "miasma" – mists that come out of the ground at night and at dawn.

'Now in fact I know from medical history that Percival Pott, famous from Pott's Fracture, had fallen off his horse in the Strand one day and got a compound fracture of his tibia. And he decided he wasn't going to have his leg amputated; instead he just wrapped it all up, and he survived it. And this was in the 1760s. So clearly, Sir Astley Cooper (the famed surgeon whom Dr Harrison had heard lecture at Guy's Hospital) knew it was possible to save a limb. It was the birth of a conservative approach.'

Famed surgeon Sir Astley Cooper.

Heidi: 'I've always been interested in the way that medicine moves on after warfare – soldiers' injuries seem to advance medical understanding – and I asked Martin about this because we were not very long after the Napoleonic Wars. And Martin explained the role that ice would have played in reducing the bleeding, because a lot of that campaign took place during the winter. So we came up with the idea that the wound might be packed in ice – that might be part of Dr Harrison's revolutionary procedure.

'Martin then described how this operation would take place using special needles and I thought that was good because Dr Harrison would have to go to Manchester to get them. So that ups the stakes, because turning a book into drama is all about seeing people *doing* things, not hearing about them after the event. I liked the idea of ice because I thought we might place an icehouse somewhere in the district so we could draw other people from the community into the drama.'

By locating the icehouse on the Hanbury estate, we were able to introduce into this storyline characters that originated in *My Lady Ludlow*. We decided it would be Mr Carter who helps transport the injured Jem to Dr Harrison's house and, upon hearing of the need for ice, commandeers Harry Gregson into helping him fetch it from Hanbury, an event which seeds the friendship that will gradually develop between these two.

Filming the Sequence

Simon Curtis: 'We've all seen countless hospital scenes, but to film an operation taking place on a kitchen table when it's a matter of life or death was rather wonderful. And the noise of the cracking bones was a very easy cue to give to the seven actresses waiting in the next-door room. When we cut to them, I loved how each of them did a completely different reaction to that agonising sound.'

Martin Scurr: 'It was only in about 1840 that they began to suture things with catgut. Prior to that, they used to glue little strips of parchment across wounds. So I got some very, very old curved needles and showed Simon Woods how to tie a surgeon's knot. And so we threaded one up and did a little practice, first with a shoelace, and then we used a bit of catgut. I probably showed Simon about twice, and then he could do it. It was a very impressive thing, that he'd grasped how to do it so quickly, and made it look so realistic.

The friendship between Harry Gregson and Mr Carter has an unlikely start when they go to fetch ice for Jem's wounds.

Andy Buchan emerges from the make-up trailer sporting a very life-like injury.

'I suggested that we meet early on the day of filming and practise the stitching – on a leg of lamb.'

The runner was asked to arrive that morning with three legs of lamb and instructed to buy the cheapest available. Unfortunately, the cheapest he found were frozen! A hairdryer from the make-up department was pressed into service and did the trick just in time.

Simon Woods: 'We practised stitching in the dressing room. I practised and practised, so that it looked as though I genuinely knew how to do it. I remember the meat being pink and fleshy, and rather disgusting actually. In fact, in the sequence, it is a leg of lamb that I am stitching – carefully kept just out of shot. It became even more disgusting as the day went on.'

Ben Smithard (on the camera): 'We shot on the Panavision Genesis system, which has the same-sized chip as the 35mm camera, so it has that Big Movie look. It enables me to shoot in really low light with candles or gas lamps and not use any other artificial light. I wanted the audience to feel that they have been taken back to the early 1840s, yet able to see every little detail in that beautiful filmic way.'

Candles

With the stories closely woven together, a chance remark by Martin opened up yet another exciting possibility for dramatising the values that the community holds dear.

Heidi Thomas: 'It led to something that became like a symbol of the town itself. Martin said: "A surgeon must have light." It was, quite literally, a light bulb moment. And I thought: "This world was so dark. There's this young doctor who has to do this incredibly difficult operation and he can't afford the candles; he can't afford the light source that he needs to work by."'

By this point in the story we had already emphasised that candles were a luxury item and that their use was strictly rationed. The ladies would rather jeopardise their eyesight than light a second candle. So how might they react when they learned of Dr Harrison's crisis of light?

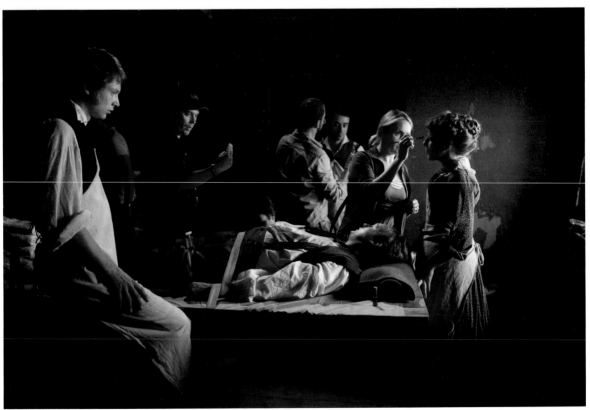

Heidi: 'I realised this would be an opportunity to see the ladies of the town bringing him their candles, thereby welcoming him to Cranford and showing him what that community is all about. It became one of those very organic *Cranford* moments, where you have maybe three beautiful elements and you can tie them together in this lovely bow that becomes something that is so much more than the sum of its parts.'

Kate Harwood, Controller of Drama Series and Serials, BBC: 'Something you really want to happen in drama is when an immense amount of work, and layering, and attention to detail at every stage ends up looking effortless. It's the most difficult thing to achieve, and one of the things I love most about *Cranford*. When I watch it now, I don't see the work; it just looks so easy. I think very few dramas manage to pull that off. It gives it a kind of confidence and effervescence that makes pretty well everything else start to feel a little bit earthbound in comparison. For the BBC, *Cranford* is a jewel in the classic crown. It is the last of a certain kind of period drama and an exemplar of it.'

Dr Harrison: 'Nothing like this is ever done in London.' Miss Deborah: 'You are not in London, Dr Harrison. You are in Cranford.'

◦⧉ The Turban ⧉◦

THERE IS A WISP of a story strand in *Cranford* that might pass unnoticed on first viewing: Matty's longing for a turban. It piqued our interest when scripting because Matty is almost universally good but, in this quest, Gaskell cleverly marks out the few times when Matty is peeved. We decided to thread it through both series. When Mary thwarts her attempt to buy a turban for the garden party, Matty's disappointment is apparent, but it is her recurrent incidental references to this that illustrate her irritation. She is then prevented from buying a tartan turban to welcome Lady Glenmire. In the final episode, when she is sad, thinking of Christmas alone, a parcel arrives from Mary, enclosing her first published story and a turban in sea-green silk, Matty's favourite colour. She wears it for the final scene. We were thus able to tie up both Mary's narrative and this wisp that had entranced us.

Miss Matty gets her wish at last.

❖❧ The Railway ❧❖

CRANFORD IS a community that feels besieged by change on many fronts – education, industrialisation, immigration, medicine. Some characters, like Deborah Jenkyns, are unwilling or incapable of adapting to these modernising forces and perish. Others, like Matty, are able to flourish because of their eventual willingness to accept change while still holding on to the values of community they most treasure. As the stories were developed across both series, we looked for ways to dramatise this theme in the most powerful and dynamic way possible. We found it in the railway. 'What I loved in the original Storylining Bible was that the railway was there as this powerful metaphor for change,' says Heidi Thomas. 'And I think why it is so apt is that the railway is such a physically frightening and transformative and unstoppable thing. And change itself is physically transforming and unstoppable and physical. As Miss Pole says: "It will power towards us like a bull that cannot be stopped."'

The public's fear of the railway was a popular subject for cartoons of the period.

The original series of *Cranford* unfolds over a calendar year, so we decided that it was unrealistic to imagine that the Cranford branch line could be planned, built and opened within our story year of 1842–3. But this suited the material very well, for it was the *fear* of what the railway might bring – imagining and anticipating the horror of it – which causes so much distress amongst the Amazons and other traditionalists in the town. We decided to dramatise just two aspects of the impending railway that hint at the scale of what is to come.

The first decision was to show a beautiful stretch of untouched countryside being marked up by the railway surveyors, in readiness for the explosives teams to begin making the cutting for the line. It is this process which fascinates young Harry Gregson when he is taken to see it by Mr Carter, and which so appals Lady Ludlow.

The Railway Dragon

Donal Woods: 'The land we were using as the Cheshire countryside was protected, so we weren't able to make any marks on it. Sue asked me to find a straightforward and vivid way to show what the coming of the railway would mean to that landscape. I suggested two simple rows of white tape on metal spikes, running parallel like railway lines, coming from over the distant hill, cutting across this rural idyll. We trusted that the audience would use their imagination and be able to picture the railway that would surge forward.'

Later scenes showed the same landscape with a huge chunk cut out from the hill, through which the lines would be laid. Not a blade of grass was harmed: the cutting was done on computer by the special effects team.

The second important visual was the Railway Works – the command centre where Captain Brown manages the planning of the line and the navvies who are building it. Donal and Richard May found the ideal location in a Hertfordshire quarry. 'I suppose we worked backwards by first finding a landscape that had already been affected by man and then

The surveyors mark the route the railway line will take.

The camera team use a locked-off camera on top of a tower to capture the extent of the Railway Works (see overleaf). The scene will be shot three times from the same position.

To keep costs down, the same extras are used three times doing different jobs in three different marked areas. In post-production the shots will be merged to make it seem as if there are many more workers.

inserting our Railway Works into it,' says Donal. 'It was important to show what a mess the railway had made of the countryside and the quarry certainly did that. We wanted the audience to be aware of the progression from cutting through this green and pretty hillside to the noise and mud of the Works.'

The Railway Arrives

When the story opens in the sequel, the railway line is destined for Chester. The only remaining question is whether or not Cranford will be part of it – a question which Heidi, Sue and Susie puzzled over during many a long script conference. 'We started with a continuation of the idea that the railway is coming and everything will be ruined,' recounts Heidi. 'And then I was sitting one day working on Miss Matty's story arc – she had changed as a character and we wanted to make sure we had depicted the new stronger Miss Matty who had moved on, just as Cranford had moved on – and I kept on thinking "It doesn't work; it's not right that the railway is going to spoil everything." And I suddenly realised that the thing that would really destroy Cranford was if the railway *never* came.'

This made sense of all of the main story threads, because the town is already in decline. Since Dr Harrison departed and Dr Morgan retired, the town has not been able to attract a doctor to live and work there. Miss Matty laments the fact that little weaving is done in Cranford any more. And two of its brightest and most capable young men – carpenter Jem Hearne and aspiring engineer William Buxton – feel thwarted by the lack of local enterprise and look for opportunities elsewhere. Miss Matty's natural affinity with the young, and her ties with Jem and William in particular, allow her to see that the town will wither and die if it loses its younger generation.

From these discussions came the idea that the ladies, urged by Matty, must be given the moment where they confront the modern age directly – by going on their first railway excursion, which would be the most exciting and frightening thing that had ever happened to them. But this meant we needed a real train and an appropriate piece of track to film it. So Sue phoned Donal with a daunting question that began: 'What if…?' With remarkable sang-froid Donal replied: 'Give me an hour.' He rang back forty minutes later to say there were two possible locomotives and several possible lines. It would be a challenge certainly, but it was feasible. Heidi remembers the excitement of that moment: 'Once we heard that, it was "all systems go" because it worked artistically, it worked emotionally, it worked historically, and it was going to work mechanically.'

Finding a Historic Railway

For Donal and Richard, the crucial first task was to find the best period locomotive that was still in working order, and a suitable track running through rural Cheshire-like countryside. Their search led them up to Cumbria and across to Newcastle before they settled on the beautifully preserved engine, the *Bellerophon*, at the Foxfield Railway in Staffordshire. Originally built to haul coal from a local colliery, the line runs for nearly four miles through rural countryside and boasts not only a brick bridge, which was ideal for filming Harry Gregson's jump on to the train, but also a small platform, which Richard realised would be perfect as the simple Hanbury Halt: 'We always thought we'd have to build a mock platform, so when we stumbled across their fantastic little platform in the middle of nowhere, we couldn't believe our luck.'

The Foxfield line operated until the mid 1960s, at which point a group of rail enthusiasts formed a preservation society in order to restore and protect it. Ron Whalley, who joined the group in 1967 as a volunteer and is now Operations Director, organised a remarkable and enthusiastic team of Foxfield volunteers to support the filming: 'Whatever the *Cranford* team wanted in terms of facilities we were able to say, "Yes, we can do that." And when they got on site they found that because we are a very rural railway, there's an awful lot of it where you can film without any of the trappings of modern life.'

The logistics of servicing a large film crew on location are always complex, but, as Rupert Ryle-Hodges notes, filming at a remote railway line is time-consuming and requires extra patience and occasional ingenuity: 'We ended up being spread-eagled across the railway line – the unit base at one end in a colliery car park, and our filming location a quarter of the way along the line. We were very fortunate at Foxfield because they had a small diesel train, which we were able to use to ferry catering, actors and the crew to and from the set. In fact, on one day we had so much rain that the roads were impassable by four-wheel-drive vehicles, and so the only way we could actually feed everyone was to have boxed lunches ferried in by the diesel train. It's not how we would conventionally do it.'

Filming the Excursion

To plan the filming of the ladies' first-ever excursion by railway, Donal drew a detailed storyboard of the sequence. Because carriages from that period did not have a corridor, we realised that there would be nowhere for the camera team to mount the camera to shoot the interiors. The solution was to build the interior in Ealing Studios, where sides could be removed as needed to make access for the camera.

For the exterior shots of the train, the *Bellerophon* was coupled up to two well-preserved period carriages from the Tanfield Railway near Newcastle, which were transported down to the Foxfield line. The construction team spent over a day measuring the historic carriages in very fine detail so that the studio-built ones would match. 'We knew that

given the time and space, it was going to be examined by the camera very closely,' says Donal. 'Sometimes you can get away with things not being exact, but we knew this wouldn't be the case.'

Building the set in the studio allowed greater control and flexibility in filming, thereby making it more efficient and less costly. To pull off the sleight-of-hand and convince the audience that the ladies were in the real carriage, Rupert took a second unit to Foxfield to film travelling plates from the line, that were then digitally inserted into the carriage windows in post-production. 'We put cameras on a flatbed trailer and photographed the view as if it were from the compartment, so that we could then take those shots and match them to the angle that we were photographing the actors from in the built compartment. We ended up going up and down the railway shooting clean views from either side of the carriages.'

Meanwhile, Ben Smithard set to work planning the main shoot: 'The train is supposed to look completely alien to the ladies, so my brief was to try and make it as dynamic as possible. The logistics were tricky, like deciding which direction the train was going. That's not easy because we had to think about the time it'd take to turn it around.' And with no turntable at Foxfield, it called for a little ingenuity from Ron and his team: 'We actually had to find rails and sleepers to drop in the middle of the car park. Then we put the loco in the middle and drove a low loader round to the other end and put it on again, so effectively we'd turned it round. It meant we had to pick it up, put it down, pick it up, and put it down again, so it was a tricky manoeuvre.'

Sue and Susie are puzzled to see Miss Deborah standing at the end of the platform amongst the Amazons (see p.209).

Factoring in time for logistical challenges such as this is a crucial aspect of filming, as the cost of a production is calculated by taking the daily rate of everyone in the cast and crew, and then adding the costs of additional services, manpower and equipment as needed to film the day's scenes. The challenge is always to film as much as possible in as little time as possible, without compromising on either the quality or integrity of the production. In short, it was necessary to implement a twenty-first-century version of 'Elegant Economy'.

An added challenge for the *Cranford* team was that, because Foxfield was about to enter the busy summer tourist season, it was necessary to film it at the very start of the shoot. Rupert: 'It's a big pressure on everybody, so you can only consider doing something like that if you are sure you can actually achieve it. I think we'd have been very wary of doing it on the second day of the shoot if the team hadn't worked together on the first series.'

But the *Bellerophon* sprung a little surprise of her own: on the night before filming, she suddenly blew out a joint in the pressure system. Ron: 'We had a lot of literal midnight oil burning to repair it and get it back into steaming condition for the first filming day. Because of the loco's age, it's like an elderly lady, and does have a sort of temperament. We were standing with our fingers crossed for the rest of the week to make sure she didn't do anything naughty. But she actually turned up trumps.'

The months of meticulous planning and preparation paid off, and the exterior shots needed for the railway excursion were finally achieved. Ben: 'Ultimately, by racing around to different locations, we did get a lot of those shots of the train that made it feel like this huge powerful machine that would intimidate these ladies.' The addition of quantities of steam, courtesy of the *Bellerophon* and special effects in post-production, and the faces of the ladies as they see the train for the first time, ensured that we captured all we had hoped for from the location.

Filming the Interior

Once location filming was completed, the production moved to a new base at Ealing Studios, and here we shot the missing interior scenes. All the characters needed to be filmed in turn reacting to the journey. To be economical with both time and money, it was decided to build only half of the interior carriage, which would serve as both ends. So, rather than moving the camera and the backing green screen, the actors would move. Simon Curtis had to talk the actors through each step of the journey, so they could time their reactions to the specific movements of the train: 'The concept of doing a virtually wordless scene three weeks later in a studio, where we only have half of a train carriage was one of the maddest days I've ever had filming. It's testimony to the skill of the actors that it worked at all.'

When film editor Fran Parker viewed the material shot that day, she concurred: 'It was the most peculiar set of rushes I've ever seen. There are the actors sitting in a wobbly carriage, on a set with a green screen in the background – with Simon just talking all the way through it, which he had to do over, and over, and over again for each take. That was sort of remarkable in itself.'

'This was a psychological experience for these characters – their first ever train ride,' recounts Simon. 'But it's also a physical experience. I think Heidi had written it imagining it a bit like the space shuttle or Concorde taking off – their faces would go back into their skulls at the speed. And when we see the train at maximum speed, it is only going about 28 miles per hour.' But given that these ladies, at best, had only travelled on a mail coach a short distance, a train travelling at such a speed and jolting violently on the tracks would have been exhilarating and terrifying in equal measure.

The studio-built carriage with the green screen behind. With nothing for the actors to see, Simon had to talk them through the journey so they could react.

To achieve the necessary jolting motion, the special effects team built a rocking mechanism. But as Rupert recalls, the first system which utilised truck springs failed at the last minute: 'I know Special Effects had a heart-stopping moment where they had to put in a totally new rocking system on the morning of the shooting which, in the end, was achieved with air

bags.' It was a technically difficult day to synchronise the movement of the studio carriage with the train exteriors as filmed on location.

More testing still, says Rupert, was the job of matching the light from location: 'For Ben to recreate the lighting effects on the cast is a real challenge – the sense of movement as the compartment goes in and out of trees, matching the lighting to what we had on location, and also giving a sense that they were really moving and co-ordinating the moves to the cameras. Building a studio compartment really simplified our problems from a production point of view, but we handed new problems on to Ben and the post-production crew.'

In the cutting room, Fran set about weaving the multitude of shots together: 'Clearly everything was there in the performance, like Miss Matty feeling ill, and Miss Pole putting her hand up because she's worried about her optic nerve. Where it became super tricky was that the journey, which had to start with the train leaving the station and end with it coming back to it, was pretty much up for grabs. So in the cutting room we had to construct the physical journey. I would do a cut and hand it to Priya, my assistant, and she would paint in the windows with the landscape going past that the second unit had shot, because that was the only way you could tell if anything was working. Also, as the train speeded up we had to make the background go faster, and in the right direction, and in the right place in the journey – so when they go through a cutting and come out into open ground, it has to match. It was extremely complicated and time-consuming.'

Paul Hamblin, Sound Mixer, and his team then set about the intricate task of building up the post-production sound: 'Steam trains make an intrinsically interesting sound, so it's about finding what will represent the animal side of it – the physical side.' Sound Effects Editor Catherine Hodgson found sounds with the right weight to them, and Paul then built them up with bass and treble. 'I put one on the left speaker and one on the right, just out of sync, so it goes, "pah doom!" across the screen, and it gives the perception of a movement.' The sound team also worked to make the studio shots meld seamlessly with location sound (recorded by Peter Brill). 'I make special compensation if it's been filmed in the studio, by adding voices, and footsteps outside the carriage, and putting the alley-type echo to represent the platform. So we add sounds that sell the era really – like birdsong in the background while the train is hissing away.'

The Railway Crash

One of the first questions Donal needed an answer to was: 'What would
happen to the train if it collided with a cow on the track?' We knew we
wouldn't be able to turn the engine on its side, but Ron explained that
the engine would probably plough through the animal but the carriages
could derail and fall to one side. Donal: 'That was invaluable information,
because we needed to know how much damage would have been done.
The train wouldn't have been smashed to pieces in a James Bond way. So
we set about building the two passenger carriages – copying them and
then laying them on their side with smashed windows, but not much other
damage. The boiler explosion at the end is probably more unexpected
because we hadn't gone too James Bond earlier.'

Having determined the nature of the crash, Donal set about drawing
up a storyboard: 'When you get sequences which are complicated and are
done in various locations with different technologies you need to write it
all down as a discussion document to bring out the problems and break
down how to do it.' He and Ben went through it together, shot by shot,
determining what should be filmed on location and what should be put on

As the carriages
had to be turned
over in the crash
and then climbed
on by the cast,
the construction
team built replicas
to required safety
standards.

the stages. Ben: 'The key is to build up tension as it goes along – Harry
running, the cow heading on to the tracks, William on the horse, Harry
jumping off the bridge – and it would need lots of shots to make it work.
Pre-planning is the key.'

The other major issue for Ben and his camera team was the time of
day of the shooting. Because it was necessary for the audience to see the
build-up to the crash, it was determined that the crash itself would happen
during daylight hours, and the crash aftermath – when Miss Galindo and
Reverend Hutton go in search of Harry – at night.

Ben: 'We decided to do a lot at dusk because you see more detail that
you can play with. But you have to avoid the sky, so we had a few matte
paint effects from Visual Effects to cover the times we couldn't avoid it.
These can be really useful. For example, if you need a dramatic sky in
a scene and you get to the location and find it's cloudy and dull, you lock
the camera in its position and trace a line around the character – ideally
they aren't moving around much – and then you remove the background
and replace it with whatever background you like. Without that help

from Visual Effects later, we would have struggled on delivering all the required elements of the railway crash.'

In the cutting room, Fran worked to assemble these shots so that the tension is ratcheted up as it heads for the moment of impact: 'I felt that it was important to describe the geography, so the impression is given that everything is moving to the same place at the same time. The key shot for this is where William rides by in the foreground, and in the background is the train. It was such a difficult shot to achieve in terms of the timing of it on location, so we fiddled with it in the cutting room. We separated out the top half of the frame from the bottom half and in this way got William riding in a little earlier than he was actually doing. And that shot in many ways is something that describes the moment really clearly: they are both heading for the same spot at speed. If you have those as a hinge, then you work everything else around it.'

To pull off the sleight-of-hand of convincing the audience that they've seen a crash without filming the actual moment of impact, it was necessary to do a locked-off shot of the cow. Fran: 'It's that fundamental thing in creating a crash. You put something where it actually didn't exist.' To achieve this, Ben framed the camera to take a shot of the cow wandering on to the track. Then without moving the camera in any way, the cow was removed and a shot was taken of the train steaming through the same track. It was a nerve-racking moment, recounts Ron: 'I remember the cameraman saying, "Is he going to be able to stop before he gets to us?" I said, "Well, we'll do several runs to see how fast he can go and where he needs to stop before he hits us." Then he explained how much the camera costs. It's probably worth more than the locomotive. I said, "If you see me jump over the hedge that side, you have my permission to jump over the hedge on the other side, if it starts going wrong."'

Fran: 'We used a lovely zooming shot at the end to heighten the emotion. And to emphasise the monstrous nature of the train, we felt that it shouldn't be a smooth zoom. So I broke it up and used every alternate frame and then zoomed in on the frames themselves so it became a juddery, fractured thing right into a big close-up of the cow and William shouting "No!"'

In post-production, the work of Paul's sound team was vital in polishing the whole sequence: 'If you were inexperienced you'd say "A train – let's make it as big and loud as we can!" But what you'd find then is that you don't have any room for the main bit – the train hitting the cow and turning over. Also, you wouldn't hear other important things that help with the building of tension, like the horse neighing. So it's all about holding back; trying to keep the sense of the train in its natural place and sort of cheating it back so you've got some room for the impact. I had some big bass things for that moment – the "boomph" sound – and you can never quite make these loud enough.'

A Bracing Start

For actor Tom Hiddleston the railway crash was not only the climactic scene in his character's story, but his first day of filming on *Cranford*. 'It was a really spectacular and epic way to start filming, for William particularly, because the whole journey of his character seemed to be about energy and progress and looking forward. He's been beating his fists against the table to get his father to support the railway and, through him, get the town to support it: "Never mind Cambridge; never mind law; never mind politics. I'm going off to be an engineer. I'm going off to work for Brunel. I'm going to get behind this fantastic thing that is the steam engine." And suddenly that very thing has almost taken the life of his beloved.

Peggy reaches up to William from the interior of the carriage; this was shot at Ealing Studios several weeks later than the crash.

'It was a big moment; a big scene for everybody on the crew. Technically, I had to canter in and stop on a specific mark, jump off the horse, jump over the railway tracks without tripping up, run around on a specific angle, climb up the side of the train, meet Edward on top of the carriage, have a little tussle with him – without either of us falling off – and then look for Peggy. And I had to do that sequence nine or ten times in this winter overcoat that felt like it weighed about three stone. And it was the hottest day of the summer, and I had to pretend it was freezing cold. But I just loved that. That's what I love about being an actor: the physicality of it. You're jumping into a situation where the stakes are incredibly high and your imagination has to work overtime. It was a great way to start; one of my favourite days.'

The Jump

From the moment the constables are called out to search for Edward
Bell, we knew the tension and pace must build until the moment when
the train hits the cow. A BBC Drama budget doesn't allow for fancy
Hollywood tricks, so we had to make this work through storytelling and
our characters. The success of the crash sequence depends on all the
elements of it moving ever faster towards meeting at the same point.

A lot of short scenes were written to be intercut, the scenes getting
briefer as the pace accelerated: Peggy decides Edward must escape to
Canada; she will go with him. Harry runs away from Miss Galindo's.
Peggy tells Matty her plans and leaves a note for William. Edward and
Peggy pack their bags. Matty tries to find William at the navvy camp.
Harry steals milk from the cow and accidentally untethers her. Mr Buxton
puts Peggy and William on the train. The cow wanders free. The train
sets off. William mounts his horse and gallops to stop Peggy leaving.
Harry hears the whistle and runs towards it. These elements are repeated

*William calls down
to Peggy from the top
of the overturned
carriage. This was
filmed on location
and intercut with
the studio-filmed
carriage interiors
of Peggy.*

several times – train/horse/Harry/cow – the cuts getting faster, until they all meet at the same second in the moment of impact. Immediately after the crash, we wanted a few seconds of silence and so cut away to Matty and Captain Brown at the navvy camp. This is a frozen moment before the chaos of the aftermath.

Harry's sequence was filmed in no less than four different places over three different months. He first ran away from Miss Galindo's house, which was in Lacock. The next shot of him hearing the train whistle and running to catch the train was filmed on June 1st – our first day of shooting – in fields in Derbyshire. Climbing on to the railway bridge and having landed in the log wagon was filmed near Stoke-on-Trent. The actual jump was shot on a mocked-up bridge at Pinewood Studios at the beginning of August.

Fourteen-year-old Alex Etel, who played Harry, explains: 'I didn't have to climb on the edge of the real bridge while the train sped underneath. Some steps had been built behind the bridge wall and I just had to walk up those and stop at the top. I was in front of the camera so it looked as if

I was balancing on the edge of the bridge as the train approached. I still had to wear a body harness, so I wouldn't fall off the steps, even though they weren't very high.'

The camera – without Harry in shot now – was then mounted on the bridge and the train was shot several times speeding towards the bridge and going under it. The next shot was to be from the other side of the bridge, looking down and seeing the train speed out with Harry lying unconscious on the logs.

While the camera was mounted on the other side, Alex was positioned lying on top of the logs in the wagon. This part was shot several times and, for every take, the train had to be backed far down the line in order to get up enough speed for when it was going under the bridge.

Alex picks up the story: 'The director and the camera crew all climbed into the log wagon to film the next bit, which was where I had to wake up. There was no dialogue, so they didn't record sound. The train travelled all the way down the line while Simon talked me through what to do, and Ben filmed it. I had to look as if I'd lost my bearings for a bit, and rub my face and then finally sit up and look pleased that I had escaped.

'It was ages later when I had to do the proper jump. They had built a huge scaffolding tower on one of the outdoor lots at Pinewood Studios. Nrinder (Dhudwar), the stunt man, had piled up lots of cardboard boxes underneath with crash mats on the top and the design team had put a kind of painted poster round the scaffolding that from the front made it look like the railway bridge. Behind this was the ladder to get up to the top.

'I climbed up the ladder with Nrinder so I could get used to how high it was, because I'm really not great with heights. At first it seemed quite high and I was a bit scared, to be honest. But Nrinder was with me all the time and there were plenty of people round the crash mats to make sure I would be safe. I was given a few tips on how to do it and I had a few practice jumps and it felt OK. So they started to film it and it just got like second nature in the end; it was really fun!'

Miss Galindo finds an unconscious Harry near the crash site and fears that he is dead.

❧ The Wedding Party ☙

FOLLOWING THE surprise wedding of Captain Brown to Lady Glenmire, invitations to an evening party are sent to their friends. Mrs Jamieson and Miss Pole, both hurt in their different ways by the wedding, refuse. But Matty, Mrs Forrester and Miss Tomkinson are pleased to celebrate the event: 'Two people of our own age, married!'

Heidi Thomas: 'I did want to mark out this little wedding party with something special. I thought that Captain Brown, being so fond of Dickens, would probably read something. And I wanted to hear Jim Carter reading *A Christmas Carol* in his beautiful, booming voice! We thought it would be entirely appropriate for Mrs Forrester to sing at the party; there's a very strong sense of her as a pretty, coquettish young woman who received a great deal of male attention at one time.'

Julia McKenzie was surprised when she read the script: 'I was a little nervous when I saw I had a song. I'm a trained opera singer so have a "placed voice" and it's hard for me to sound folksy and untrained. So composer Carl Davis and I tried different keys to make it sound more like Mrs Forrester. I always saw her as rather shy, but people did entertain each other at parties then, and this was a very emotional evening for her – two friends newly married, and she a widow; I think this is why she is happy to stand up to sing.'

Jim Carter reading from A Christmas Carol *gives as much pleasure to the cast as Captain Brown does to his wedding guests.*

Julia McKenzie singing a solo as Mrs Forrester, accompanied by Celia Imrie, who had to be taught to play the piece.

Heidi found a song in a secondhand copy of a book of old English ballads. It had no music, but we knew that Carl would write something to fit in with the *Cranford* score. The song, 'All Alone', is about someone moving from love into loneliness and then into old age. Heidi: 'Although a new marriage was being celebrated, there was a sense that Cranford was moving into darker days. Old friends are not speaking, Mr Buxton is estranged from his son, there's a love story that is not going as it should, and an emotional undertow that the ladies who were once the young belles in Cranford are inching towards old age. We didn't want a song that was too explicit, but something that could sit under a montage both of the faces of the people in the room, and the ones who have excluded themselves and are alone.'

Underclothes and Overheating

WEARING PERIOD costumes that are historically accurate can help an actor to understand the character and the social mores of the world he or she inhabits. But, on a practical level, they can be burdensome and occasionally uncomfortable. Invariably, they involve more layers – in the case of the female characters, many more.

A petticoat frame, not yet in fashion in Cranford.

Simon Woods checks out Lisa Dillon's 'duvet' petticoats.

Ben uses massed candles, just out of shot, instead of film lights.

Jenny Beavan: 'In the 1840s, everybody wore corsets. To us, it would feel very odd, but it was completely natural to them. Girls were put into them at puberty so they were used to feeling constrained by clothes. The corsets would be worn over a cotton chemise, which could be easily washed. Knickers weren't worn; there were some bloomery things beginning to come in, but it wasn't normal. There would be a petticoat or two, one possibly padded with feathers to give a bell-shape outline. In winter, a red flannel petticoat would be added for warmth. They would wear woollen stockings held up by garters and little boots. Over that underwear came the dress for which there would be a variety of lace collars and tippets, inner

sleeves and outer sleeves, belts and little shawls. A lady was never seen without a cap, even in bed, from the time she was married or of a certain age. Bonnets were worn on top of the cap when going out, with cloaks, large shawls and mittens.'

Of course, in the 1840s, houses had very little heating so these layers might have been essential. But on the stages of London's film studios – with the sealed doors, thick sound-proof walls, many lights, enclosed candle-lit sets and stacks of real candles just off-screen that Ben Smithard used to give the softly flickering effect of candlelight – the heat was intense. Imagine all this for the final scene in the Assembly Rooms which was filmed on one of the hottest days of the year, and add to that space the entire main cast plus some extras, a small band and a very large crew, and then ask the cast to dance again and again. And again. And to enjoy it.

⊰ The Assembly Rooms ⊱

I

N THE NOVEL, there is only a brief mention of the Assembly Rooms, when the ladies go there to see Signor Brunoni's magic show, but it is a very potent paragraph. Gaskell mentions a 'dusty recollection of the days that were gone' lingering about the place and has Miss Matty giving 'a sigh or two to her departed youth'.

Heidi Thomas: 'This resonated with a personal experience. When I was eighteen in Liverpool, there was a fire one night which completely destroyed the Rialto Ballroom where my mother had danced as a girl. She was so upset that I went with her to see the ruins. There were many women of her age doing the same thing: going back to the Ballroom of Romance. I remember my mother bending down to pick up a little ceramic tile in the shape of a cupid's head and saying: "This was in the ladies' room where we went to put on our lipstick and smoke." It was the spirit of this that I wanted to recreate when our Amazons walk into the Assembly Rooms; that they are crossing the threshold back to their lost youth.'

Peter Jenkyns's attire has many hints of his time in India.

Once the centre of Cranford's winter social life, where the county families gathered to play cards and dance, the Assembly Rooms above the George Inn have long since been closed. In Series One we chose not to refer to them. But, during our scripting discussions for the sequel, the potential for the Rooms to link several story strands grew more persuasive.

The disused and dilapidated Rooms became a metaphor for the atrophy of the town; there was no work for the young people and no public places for entertainment. We resolved that it would be Matty – 'undecided' Matty – who would be the force behind the scheme to rescue and refurbish the Rooms, in the hope of repairing the rift in the town. And so our one scene grew into five, which had to bear the weight of substantial story moments. This turned the Assembly Rooms into a significant location for the design department to realise.

The ladies look back in time. It takes the combined skills of all departments to create the nostalgic atmosphere.

Scene 2/44: Int. Day. The Assembly Rooms.

The lock is beginning to give way — the soft wood buckles and splinters as the doors open inwards. As they do so, a small portion of ceiling plaster collapses, giving rise to a shower of dust.

When the miasma of powdered dirt settles, the chamber is revealed. Light streams through dirty windows, slicing through an elegantly proportioned room. We see faded salmon plaster, a wooden floor. There is a framed mirror on one wall, an empty fireplace on the other. Cobwebbed sconces bear the merest stumps of candles, and half a dozen fractured chairs are evident, their gilded paintwork furred with dust.

Miss Pole, Miss Matty and Mrs Forrester half-reach for each other's hands as they creep over the threshold. It is almost as though they expect to hear music. The room appears to hold them in its web of dust-strung air. They look about them, as if expecting to encounter their own ghosts.

MRS. FORRESTER

Matches were made in this chamber once.

Miss Matty's old dance card, copied from an original.

The Ballroom of Romance

Simon Curtis: 'Filming the ladies returning to the Assembly Rooms, I was reminded of a quotation from F. Scott Fitzgerald: "There's a time full of the promise of happiness which is subsequently realised as the happiness itself." And that was this moment for them; what the scene was all about.'

Heidi Thomas: 'I deliberately kept the comments from the ladies very restrained, building towards the moment with the three of them looking in the mirror. Miss Pole, noticing the mottled glass, says: "They are the specks of age," but is really talking about the marks of age on their faces.'

Donal Woods: 'The script called for the Assembly Rooms to be derelict the first time they are seen, and then totally refurbished for the Christmas party. In story terms, those occasions are weeks apart. In our filming reality, it was two days later. Georgian Assembly Rooms are few and far between in the UK and one wouldn't be allowed to break them down as

we needed. The decision was made to build on the stage at Ealing Studios, giving more control over what we could do. And a bonus was the original wooden floor, worn and pitted from films like *Kind Hearts and Coronets*.'

Ben Smithard: 'When the ladies visit the Assembly Rooms after so many years, I wanted the scene to feel nostalgic; not old-fashioned, just nostalgic. So I made it warm, which is something I hadn't done before in *Cranford*. The shot where the three ladies are looking in the mirror is one of my favourite shots. You probably wouldn't notice, but as we see Matty wiping the dust from the mirror, I turned the lighting back to slightly more neutral, so it would seem as if she's going into her own world.'

Fran Parker: 'What I particularly liked about the scene was the final tableau shot, the wide shot of the three ladies and the mirror. The composition and lighting are so exquisite that I wanted to hold the shot for as long as possible, with the music drifting away. So what you are left with is a very painterly arrangement; they seem frozen in time, like a Vermeer.'

Miss Matty wipes the dust from the mirror and recalls her younger self in love with Mr Holbrook, a moment Ben emphasises with a subtle change of lighting.

The opening description of the Assembly Rooms in the script. (Top left)

Carl Davis: 'This was the setting where courtships had started and promises had been made and broken. Even though it's dusty and faded, there's a particular atmosphere as soon as the ladies enter; it's shimmering and mysterious. And I thought this is where we should introduce the first hint of the waltz, but in a distant way, prefiguring what will happen later.'

Imelda Staunton: 'For the three Cranford ladies, looking in the mirror was a trip down Memory Lane. But, of course, it's interesting thinking about the three of us too. For me, it was both the character and the actor looking into the mirror. I had seen Judi playing Lady Macbeth at the Young Vic in 1977 and remember thinking: "I'll never be as good as that. That's amazing." Around the same time, long before I understudied Julia McKenzie, I noticed that she was in a musical at a theatre I was passing and thought: "Oh, I'll go and see that." I got a seat at the very back of the Circle and she just blew me away. So, looking in that mirror, I was thinking: "Here I am with these two amazing women who I knew before they knew me." It was poignant for me on a very personal level as well as for my character.'

The Magic Show

Tim Curry: 'Simon had given me the boxed set of *Cranford* and I watched it straight through. Then I just went back to PLAY and watched it again. I was obsessed with it. I called my agent and said: "If they ever do another *Cranford*, I want you to *beg* for me to be in it. I don't care about humiliation. I want to be in it."'

As it happened, he was perfect casting for Signor Brunoni, the magician who comes to town for the Christmas Eve party. But, as Tim lives in Los Angeles, he was not able to be at the rehearsals before shooting started; so he arrived and had to go very speedily through all the processes of costume fittings, a hair and make-up trial, a dance rehearsal and then work up a convincing Magic Show that he would later have to perform in front of the assembled cast.

Signor Brunoni is not Italian, as his name suggests; nor is he Indian, which his costume suggests. His theatre bill boasts that he is the 'Grand Magician of Arabia, Wizard to the King of Delhi' and that he has 'played before the Lama of Tibet'. Tim decided he probably hales from Bradford,

Signor Brunoni chooses Miss Pole to assist him. His costume and make-up were planned to give the character a slightly seedy theatricality that brings a touch of rare exoticism to Cranford.

but it's important that his audience thinks he comes from exotic parts. He adopted an outrageously exaggerated Italian accent, and Jenny Beavan gave a slightly seedy theatrical look to both his day clothes and to the robe and turban he wears for the performance. Karen Hartley-Thomas decided that his make-up – darkened skin, thick eyeliner, worn on and off stage – had to look self-applied, with a somewhat heavy hand.

It would have been possible on film to cheat all the tricks in the editing room by cutting round what he was doing on stage, but we were keen that the act was done as a magician of that period would have done it. This involved Tim in learning a series of tricks, some with a real dove, which he had to perform in real time. Working with magic consultant Paul Kieve, we had already planned the shape of the show and what the tricks would be, but Tim then had to rehearse it all in record time, learning all the sleight-of-hand skills at the same time as getting used to his costume and meeting the rest of the cast, of whom there were many.

The first whiff of the exotic we had experienced infiltrating *Cranford* was when the oranges were eaten. Carl highlighted this little scene by introducing a Moorish tango, climaxing as Matty sucks her orange in the privacy of her room, with the juice running down her chin. He decided it would be appropriate to reprise this theme for Brunoni, who has such a mongrel provenance. So, whenever he is discussed by the ladies, or when Miss Pole sneaks in to spy on his props, this music underscores the scene. We decided in story terms that he would have brought his own stage managers who would double as musicians and they would give a general background of Eastern music to his act. But any variety act will always have percussive sounds to highlight the peak of each trick. Carl suggested that we record a wide variety of percussion sounds and lay them on to Brunoni's tricks in the dubbing theatre afterwards.

Baby Tilly emerges from the magician's box.

In fact, this turned out to be the very last thing we did at the end of weeks of sound work with Paul's team. We sat very late into the last evening trying the many cymbal, gong and drum rolls that had been recorded against the pictures of Brunoni's tricks, one after the other, after the other. Each effect had been introduced on tape by the

percussionist in his East End accent and we were foolishly delighted, as the clock ticked to midnight, that the final sound we put on to *Cranford* was from the Burmese Nipple Gong.

Tim Curry: 'To be on the stage, performing for the entire cast – all these starry actors – was a bit scary. But the Magic Show was all about presentation, brio and bravura. And that I can do. I just delivered my usual 300lb of condemned ham and enjoyed it!'

Imelda Staunton: 'Oh, being chosen to assist in the Magic Show by Signor Brunoni – it's the best night of her life! She's never been chosen for anything in her life before. And then to be singled out by this magnificent man – the most extraordinary man Cranford has ever seen. It's very stirring for her. She's the last person you'd expect to be swept away, but I think it shows her deep-buried longing for romance that has had no opportunity to flourish. But then suddenly to have this wonderful and exotic being make her feel special. I found it touching that she could be so floored by this man.'

Imelda is as thrilled to work with Tim as part of the Magic Show as her character is to assist Signor Brunoni.

The Waltz

Carl Davis: 'It seemed to me that the Assembly Rooms was always going to be the climax, so my first job was to find the waltz. Once you have the tune, you can have the dance.'

Jane Gibson: 'I was asked a long time in advance: if we were to have a Christmas dance, what might it be? And we talked about the waltz and how it might suit the narrative line of adapting to new things because, although the waltz had been danced for many years in London, it might not have reached Cranford. And it was decided that to see it happening for the first time would be a very visual, physical way of showing through people's bodies what was happening historically; that people were opening out a little bit.'

Heidi had threaded the idea of the waltz as something rather scandalous through the scripts and, as she worked on the ending, the brief became clearer. We would see particular pairings for this novel dance: Matty with Mr Buxton, friends once more; Peggy and William, with his arm still bandaged, but together at last. Each couple highlighting a part of the stories we had seen them live through. But we also wanted to emphasise the cohesion of the town and the many relationships. So it was decided that, at a certain point in the waltz, the dancers would open naturally into a circle, a perfect symbol of unity and harmony, and dance as one. They would move amongst each other so we could observe the different associations, and would then return to their original partner for the end of the dance.

Carl: 'We worked out the musical shape of the dance in my sitting room, with me on piano and Jane and Sue dancing various figures on the floor. We had to work out exactly how many bars were needed and what would be happening in them. As the dance would lead into the final credits, we decided to segue into the *Cranford* theme tune – in waltz time – at the point where they open to dance with each other.'

Jane: 'We wanted it to look as if this was not a familiar dance, so I gave each couple a different way of holding each other. But when they danced as a town, I shifted to a quadrille, a figure dance they would have all known. What's really unusual is that every person in the dance is a recognised character. Normally, there will be a few principal actors and the rest will be dancers. So that was exciting, but logistically it is impossible to have twenty leading actors together at the same time to rehearse before filming starts. So some were only taught the dance on the day of filming, in the only available space – the dining tent!'

Ben Smithard: 'How the camera works in a choreographed sequence can be tricky. Usually, with something like this, it would be on the outside, so you can see the pattern of the dance. But towards the end of the sequence I thought something was quite wrong and I realised we needed to be right in the middle with the camera. If you don't feel the music when you're moving the camera, it's going to be wrong.'

Fran Parker: 'What made it so pleasurable to cut is that the camera is right in the heart of the dance. The characters swing past the camera, which is dynamic, and I could swing from one character to another. It gave it a lot more energy. The brief was to see everybody in character, because this is really the curtain call before the final lines from Mr Buxton and Matty.'

The final scene: the main characters of the town join together to dance the waltz.

Jane: 'People always assume that actors can't dance, but that's not the case. Judi was very featured in the dance and she's just a master at absolutely everything; she creates an atmosphere around her. The way she works is very focused but she's very light. And she was dancing with Jonathan Pryce, who has done a lot of musicals and he really knows how to dance.'

Carl: 'On screen we see the quartet on stage play the waltz for the people dancing in that room; it's very realistic. But as the scene develops, the music has a different role, which is that it must help to tell the story. So the music for the dance becomes part of the score for the film, and then you can take artistic licence and step away from realism. As the shots open up to the full ballroom, we're looking for an emotional response to what is happening to the characters. So the music can take more weight and get fuller. We're producing this very consciously in post-production by adding a dozen more instruments at this point, but we're looking for an instinctive response to it, not an intellectual one: a response that draws people into the emotion of the ending of this story.'

Jonathan Pryce: 'The Assembly Rooms dance was a great pleasure and made me realise how much I enjoy that kind of formal dancing. I'll have a waltz to do on a film occasionally, and I'll certainly dance on stage. But I loved the whole thing – the structured dancing, learning the routine. And it was great fun working with Judi on it because, when first learning it, we didn't always remember where to go when – we'd be taking each other by surprise. And also, I'd be bumping into Nick Le Prevost every thirty seconds; we constantly found ourselves crashing into each other. But I loved it and had a really wonderful time doing it.'

Judi Dench: 'We danced a great deal – a huge amount. I thought it was going to be unbelievably hot, but it wasn't uncomfortable. It was hugely good fun to do. We'd all learnt the dance, so it was just a question of being your character.'

Behind the Scenes

❖ Off Set ❖

SHOOTING DAYS are long, complex and full of pressures. Time is of the essence and the speed of work has to be maintained, day in day out. But there are periods during shooting where the actors must wait whilst all the other departments work rapidly to turn things round for the next shot, or while the weather does its worst. Keeping one's energy focused can be difficult, but the best actors can play as well as work. The atmosphere off set can become a barometer of the well-being of the production. The work must be taken seriously, but that doesn't mean it has to be solemn.

The paper-tearing game: the Amazons keep busy while waiting for the rain to stop.

Judi Dench: 'I loved the fact that there was so much good spirit amongst us whilst making *Cranford*. Actors don't need to have their egos stroked all the time, contrary to what everybody believes. What they want is to feel that it's a whole piece that is being done together, with everyone – cast and

crew – being equally looked after. In this way you become a company –
like a theatre company; a group that can work and play together. And
that's wonderful. You become a company of people who have the same
aim in view, and who work together to make it happen; that is, to tell the
story. After all, that is our duty to the audience.'

Fun and Games

Kimberley Nixon: 'We often had to sit under a little tent waiting for it to
stop raining, and Judi had so many games in her bag of tricks. She taught
us one game where you are given a piece of newspaper and the name of
an object, such as a car, and you rip away at the paper to make that shape.
Eileen Atkins was really bad at it – if Judi said make it a car, she'd make
something that looked more like a boat!'

Judi Dench: 'There's nothing like sitting under a tent in the rain for
bringing a company together. It was actually a big help in terms of getting
to know the actors I'd never worked with before. One time, while we
were sitting in the woods waiting to be called, everyone had to tear out
a train. We were interrupted and, while we went away to do our scene on
the real train, somebody came and thought, "What's all this rubbishy
paper doing?" and screwed it all up. Barbara Flynn was very miffed as she
was sure she was going to be the winner.'

Tom Hiddleston: 'At Ealing Studios one day while the lighting was being
changed, we were sitting around in a semi-circle quietly doing crosswords
and reading the paper, when suddenly and without warning, Judi jumped
up out of her seat and said, "What international city am I?" and started
doing a kind of mime of washing herself. Somebody said "Washington!"
Got it! So then we all had to get up and do a mime of a city in the world.
Jodie Whittaker sat crossed-legged, waved her arms about and went
"Shoo, shoo!" and that was Budapest.

'Another day, while we were waiting upstairs in the dressing rooms,
Jodie and Michelle Dockery taught me the whole of the dance from
Beyonce's "Single Ladies" video. I won't forget them performing that in
their corsets and long skirts! That was very entertaining. I had to dance
it in my britches and riding boots.'

Bake-a-cake Day

The Amazons decided a treat was in order for the crew and secretly planned a tea party. They each baked a cake and invited the crew to tea under the trees by the church. They had brought a tablecloth and even a vase of flowers. The secret was nearly out when Celia Imrie, in full Lady Glenmire costume, was spotted kneeling by the hedge, icing the chocolate cake that she had baked at four o'clock that morning.

Standards were high and the competition fierce. 'I did a Victoria sponge and a lemon drizzle cake,' says Imelda. 'Lesley Manville did lemon drizzle as well and hers was slightly superior to mine. But don't ever put that in print!'

A Trip to the Dentist

One day on set at Ealing Studios, Judi lost a crown from her tooth. It was essential to get it fixed immediately, before the close-ups. Fortunately, Karen Hartley-Thomas lived locally and fixed a lunchtime appointment with her dentist. There would not be enough time to 'de-rig' Judi, so she was taken in full costume, complete with Miss Matty wig and lace cap.

Judi Dench: 'I walked in, sat in the waiting room and everyone pretended to read their magazines. When I got in to see the dentist, he tipped the seat back and, as he started, he asked: "And are you working on anything at the moment?"'

Mittens

Jenny Beavan: 'There was a moment during the second series when Judi rather timidly asked if she could have new mittens for the final scene in the Assembly Rooms. It was such a large cast and we had so little money that I thought it best to say "no" in case everybody wanted a new pair.'

Judi Dench: 'They're woollen mittens and if you wear them for a long while, they stretch; then you find yourself picking at them and they stretch even more. But Jenny was very firm: no new mittens. So we were very spiteful if anyone had a new dress. When Celia arrived, she had a lot of very good clothes. I was furious when I saw her coming out in that tartan!'

Celia Imrie: 'My wedding costume was rather gorgeous and it had been specially made for me, whereas Judi had to wear costumes that she'd worn before. So I took great delight in showing off my new dress, much to her chagrin. She thought that I shouldn't be allowed to have such a lovely dress. She took a very dim view of me. You know, being allowed to be in Jim Carter's arms and ride on a horse and cart. She was pretty cross about that as well.'

The Company

Imelda Staunton: 'It was a great job because we had a wonderful script and a wonderful cast. And that does not often happen at the same time. But also, it did feel very special because we knew each other so well. It did feel a very close-knit community. And that was what was special for me: that it was rich work with good people.'

Julia McKenzie: 'It was so enjoyable, and I admired the other actresses so much. We just had a wonderful feeling on set: it was a lovely crew and everybody was having a good time, and that helps to make a really good product.'

Tom Hiddleston: 'The atmosphere on the set was one of the most jovial, playful and fun that I've ever experienced. There was a real sense of bonhomie and camaraderie that comes with the fact that everybody's so experienced. As a young actor it sometimes feels like quite a lonely business, going from job to job. And then you look at the people in *Cranford* and you think "Ah, these people have known each other for years. And their paths have crossed and recrossed many times. And they've worked together in theatre and they've done films together." And seeing those friendships really cemented made me look forward to a time when I would be working with people who I'd worked with many times before, with thirty years behind me.'

Jonathan Pryce: 'It was interesting to play a character that was coming into that society; what was happening to me as an actor was reflected in what was happening to the character. There was an air of expectancy about his return, and also the return of his son and his ward. So the

Heidi chats to Tom while on a visit to location.

Buxtons weren't quite "the outsiders", but they were just outside enough to spark people's interest in them again. I knew most of the actors and they made all the newcomers very welcome, and I think a lot of that is down to the way Sue runs the whole production. Obviously, there was a great deal of pressure to get a lot done in a very short amount of time, but it felt a very unpressured way to work, mainly because of the excellence of the camera crew, who were super-efficient. If filming is not quite going right, I usually try to find something positive, but I didn't have to scratch around doing *Cranford*. It was all good.'

Simon Woods: 'I felt a real affinity with Dr Harrison at times: this community of formidable women, into which the young and inexperienced man walks. There was definitely a parallel in the combination of wonder and feeling slightly intimidated, but also in feeling totally charmed by it all.'

The Spirit of Miss Deborah

WHEN EILEEN ATKINS won the BAFTA Best Actress award for her portrayal of Miss Deborah, she took time in her acceptance speech to curse us for killing off her character: 'Woe betide you if you decide to make a sequel; I will haunt you!' When we began production on *Return to Cranford*, she was true to her word. On the first morning of rehearsals when all were gathered discussing a scene, there was a tap at the door and a large crate of oranges was delivered with a note from Eileen: 'All sucking to be done in public.'

First day's rehearsal is interrupted while we all suck our oranges for a photo Simon snaps on his mobile phone to send to Eileen.

Barbara Flynn: 'She's so polite, isn't she, Eileen? It was a wonderful bit of generosity from her. I decided to make marmalade for everyone from the oranges, as a way of saying thank you to all the cast and crew. I called it

"Miss Deborah Jenkyns Memorial Marmalade". It was potted, labelled and topped with either a page of script with each character's lines of dialogue or a call sheet for the crew, and tied with a piece of string: Elegant Economy!'

Eileen's note had repeated the warning that we would not be rid of her so easily and Judi reacted to this with her characteristic sense of larkiness: 'I secretly organised with Charlotte in the costume department to have a life-size photograph of Miss Deborah (clutching her candles) mounted on a polystyrene backing, with a folding hinge at the back so she could stand independently – as of course Deborah would!' During the filming of the Amazons on the railway platform, in the first week of shooting, we all looked down to the end where the ladies were gathered and were baffled to see Miss Deborah amongst them! It took a few seconds to realise that it was not Eileen. A photograph of the group was taken and immediately dispatched to her, and the idea was born to tour the cut-out and to capture her image in as many settings as possible. Miss Deborah may have left us, but she was always with us in spirit.

Captain Brown is aware of a strange presence.

Miss Deborah refuses to be left out on the railway trip.

❧ Working with Animals ☙

ONE THING about *Cranford* that made things extra challenging for the director was that every scene not only included several leading actors, it might also contain an animal, a baby or a stunt.

Stephen Miles asked for a ten-minute warning to fasten up Bessie's pyjamas for filming. He cautioned Phil: 'Don't give a ten-minute warning if you're not going to use her for an hour, because you'll regret it!'

The Cow

'I was a little dubious when I read in the script: "Mrs Forrester walks along Princess Street with Bessie, her cow,"' says Julia McKenzie. 'Having lived in the country, I know that cows are big and can be dangerous, so I was a bit wary. But our one was like a big dog. She hit all her marks, she didn't complain, she didn't want tea breaks. I was holding her on a piece of rope and doing a rather emotional scene with Judi Dench. I had just said: "Bessie is like a daughter to me," when the cow turned towards me and laid her head very gently on my chest. Without thinking, I put my arm

round her neck and kissed her muzzle. It wasn't planned; the cow took over. It was a fantastic performance; she should have been up for a BAFTA.'

The cow's passive nature, however, posed a problem when filming the scene where she has fallen into a lime pit. Jim Carter: 'We had to imagine that the cow was thrashing around in agony in this pit of lime, whereas it was being rather docile in this pit of mud. And there's always the fear

"Am I compensating for the fact that the cow isn't doing a lot, by overacting myself?" Peter Brill was anxious that she was completely silent, so I did my renowned cow-mooing-in-distress performance, which he recorded. I am slightly aggrieved I didn't get a screen credit.'

When Mrs Forrester realises that the lime has singed off the cow's hair, she takes seriously Captain Brown's joke about it needing pyjamas, and buys a 'great quantity of flannel' from Johnson's. It fell to Costume Supervisor Stephen Miles to realise this creation: 'We weren't sure what it would look like, but the cow needed to be able to function as an animal, so it had to be a wraparound affair. I went off with a *very* long tape measure and took several rather random measurements and made a big flat-out pattern directly on cloth. We devised a method of buttons and tapes to make the finished result look like a garment that was a perfectly functioning item for a large animal to wear and walk about in. She was a very nice, elderly cow named Lily and there were no problems during her costume fitting, though I had to keep a weather eye out for what she was doing with her hooves. I had a couple of goes at perfecting what it was to look like, and to accommodate things like udders, and indeed soiling. But that's the life of a costume person – it's all glamour.'

An inert Carlo shows off his dashing scarlet coachman's coat. He had more costumes than the Amazons were allowed.

The Parrot

In *Return to Cranford* Miss Pole and Mrs Forrester set about constructing a cage for Miss Pole's parrot, only to discover later that it is a steel petticoat hoop. Before filming started, the parrot was brought to the rehearsal rooms so that the staging of the scene could be worked out. 'I'm not sure

A moment that wasn't planned. During the scene the parrot climbed up Imelda's arm and started to nibble her lace. Amazingly, she kept in character and made the shot.

who was more frightened of the parrot, me or Julia,' recounts Simon. 'In an effort to reassure her, I took hold of the cage and as soon as the parrot moved, I dropped it, which didn't help anybody.'

'I'm afraid I wasn't very good with the parrot,' admits Julia. 'I was the one supposed to hold on to the top of the petticoat cage but, when it moved swiftly upwards towards my hand, I said: "I can't do this!" So Imelda, who was only about as high as this enormous cage, had to take over. She's fearless.'

Judi also had a scene with the parrot, where she warily eyes him up while trying to remove the baby's things from his reach. 'I adored the parrot,' says Judi. 'As I edged past him, he suddenly started to bounce up and down, throwing his head back and clattering his beak. Wonderful performance! And then later when I was doing my ADR (additional recorded dialogue), I was told that the bird had to come back too, as there weren't enough parrot noises and I said: "Oh, please let me do that." Having done my scenes with the parrot, I thought: "Well, I know how you said the lines." So I auditioned there and then, and got the part!'

❖❅ The Women of Cranford ❅❖

IT'S UNUSUAL – even now – to have a production with such a prevalence of women in leading parts, both in front of the camera and in such key roles behind it.

Jim Carter: 'As a working experience, it was heaven to be surrounded by such bright and funny women. It makes a huge difference to the work environment. Crews tend to be male-dominated, especially around the camera and on the working floor, but here we had such strong women, not only in the cast but also from producer to crew. There's such an air of humour and compassion and ease when women are around; and such wonderful women! – so confident in themselves, so relaxed and able to do their jobs on the turn of a sixpence. No temperament, no side issues, no messing about. You knew from the word go that you were playing with the "A" Team.'

Waiting to be called on set: Jim enjoys a moment with some of the ladies of Cranford.

❧ Darkness Lane ❧

'THERE IS ALWAYS one scene that for some reason never settles anywhere in the schedule,' is Rupert's view. This is often known on films as the 'Telephone Box' scene. It's usually a tiny scene, involving only one or two actors and thought to be something that can be 'fitted in' on another day. So the props wagon always has the telephone box aboard and the scene is often added to the bottom of the call sheet, with the note: 'If time'. When the day is going well, the box might be unloaded and set up in some suitable place and all departments are warned that it is hoped to shoot it at the end of the day. Invariably on wrap, the box is loaded back on to the truck unused.

Darkness Lane was a short scene, maybe only thirty seconds on screen, but it caused a lot of head scratching over the weeks of production. The Amazons are leaving Mrs Jamieson's Halloween party, having scared themselves with tales of headless ghosts. We were filming in high summer

With Miss Matty in the sedan chair, the three ladies clutch their lanterns and brave Darkness Lane. We trusted the imagination of the audience to make this work.

so there was very little darkness possible in our schedule. We toured the sedan chair and at various locations we tried to find high-hedged lanes or wooded paths.

In the end, we followed Rupert's advice and shot it on a huge black empty stage at Pinewood. The sedan chair carriers were to run from one end to the other with the ladies trying to keep up, so soil was laid in a long track edged with some bushes. When Judi saw this, she exclaimed: '*Six* little bushes? We could have done it in my back garden!' But we were relying on the fact that as no one would be able to see anything much when we filled the whole stage with swirling mists, the audience's imagination – led by the reactions of the Amazons – would create for us what wasn't there.

On the first series, our 'telephone box' scene was Matty sitting in a corner of her garden, reading the letter from Mr Holbrook. Ideally, this should have been shot in the first week's filming in Lacock, but the schedule was already overloaded and Donal's reasoning was that we could create a corner of her garden anywhere. We only needed a table, a chair and a stretch of backing fence. During the following weeks of shooting around the country, we never found the time to film it. At the end of week fifteen, on our final day of filming, sure enough, the scene was on the call sheet 'to be fitted in when time'.

It had to be shot somewhere near to where the Unit was shooting, as there would be no time to move. During the day, as the Unit moved and the sun moved, Donal created Matty's garden five times in five different places. With only ten minutes of the day (and the shoot) left, a tiny unit sped a few yards up the hill to the new set, Judi took off her bonnet and changed shawls, sat in the chair, picked up the letter and Phil called 'Action!' And this very touching scene of her promising future was shot. When he announced that filming was completed, we turned around and saw that the production team had somehow silently organised everyone into position for the final cast and crew photograph (overleaf). Eileen Atkins, who had finished filming several weeks before, had secretly arrived to be part of it and Judi walked down to take her place in the company photograph.

Miss Matty reads the letter from Mr Holbrook: the final shot of the first series, filmed in the last ten minutes.

Cast and crew photograph, August 2007. (Overleaf)

Cast

Francesca Annis	Lady Ludlow
Eileen Atkins	Miss Deborah Jenkyns
Claudie Blakley	Martha
John Bowe	Dr Morgan
Andrew Buchan	Jem Hearne
Jim Carter	Captain Brown
Tim Curry	Signor Brunoni
Judi Dench	Miss Matty Jenkyns
Lisa Dillon	Mary Smith
Michelle Dockery	Erminia Whyte
Alex Etel	Harry Gregson
Emma Fielding	Miss Galindo
Deborah Findlay	Miss Tomkinson

Barbara Flynn	The Hon. Mrs Jamieson
Michael Gambon	Mr Holbrook
Debra Gillett	Mrs Johnson
Philip Glenister	Mr Carter
Selina Griffiths	Caroline Tomkinson
Tom Hiddleston	William Buxton
Hannah Hobley	Bertha
Celia Imrie	Lady Glenmire
Alex Jennings	Reverend Hutton
Rory Kinnear	Septimus Hanbury
Nicholas Le Prevost	Peter Jenkyns (C2)
Dean Lennox Kelly	Job Gregson
Emma Lowndes	Bella Gregson
Lesley Manville	Mrs Rose
Joe McFadden	Dr Marshland

Julia McKenzie	Mrs Forrester	Nicholas Bishop	Giacomo
Matthew McNulty	Edward Bell	Rosy Byrne	Lizzie Hutton
Kimberley Nixon	Sophy Hutton	Andrew Byrne	Malachi Gregson
Alistair Petrie	Major Gordon	Imogen Byron	Kate
Jonathan Pryce	Mr Buxton	Bessie Carter	Margaret Gidman
Julia Sawalha	Jessie Brown	Haydon Downing	Walter Hutton
Adrian Scarborough	Mr Johnson	Roger Ennals	Mulliner (C1)
Lesley Sharp	Mrs Bell	Adam Henderson-Scott	Auctioneer's Assistant
Martin Shaw	Peter Jenkyns (C1)	Patricia Leach	Gypsy Woman
Imelda Staunton	Miss Octavia Pole	Roddy Maude-Roxby	Mulliner (C2)
Jodie Whittaker	Peggy Bell	Hester Odgers	Helen Hutton
Finty Williams	Clara Smith	Andy Rashleigh	Mr Goddard
Greg Wise	Sir Charles Maulver	Hannah Stokeley	Bessie
Simon Woods	Dr Harrison	Chloe & Olivia Wadkin	Tilly Hearne
Rod Arthur	Auctioneer	Andrew Westfield	Farmer Graves

Crew

Created by
Sue Birtwistle and Susie
Conklin from the novels
of Elizabeth Gaskell

Written by
Heidi Thomas

Directed by
Simon Curtis

Co-producer
Rupert Ryle-Hodges

Director of Photography
Ben Smithard

Production Design
Donal Woods

Film Editors
Frances Parker ACE
Dan Roberts (C1)

Music
Carl Davis

Costume Design
Jenny Beavan

Make-up and Hair Design
Alison Elliott (C1)
Karen Hartley-Thomas (C2)

Titles Design
Posy Simmonds

Casting Director
Maggie Lunn

Choreography and Etiquette
Jane Gibson

Dubbing Mixer
Paul Hamblin

Sound Recordist
Peter Brill

Location Managers
Richard May
Jamie Lengyel (C1)

Production Consultant
Gordon Ronald

1st Assistant Director
Phil Booth

2nd Assistant Director
Ben Harrison (C1)
Harriet Worth (C2)

2nd Assistant Director, crowd
Christian Rigg (C1)
Sarah Hood (C2)

3rd Assistant Director
Hannah Brown (C1)
Danielle Bennett (C2)

Floor Runner
Gemma Read (C1)
Chris Foggin (C2)

Stand-in/Runners
Tania Gordon (C1)
Courtney Getter (C1)
Andy Hodgson (C1)
Cathy Lorimer (C2)
Ruth Keir (C2)

Unit Managers
Sharon McGuinness
Rebecca Davis (C1)

Assistant Location Manager
Sparky Ellis
Vicky Chapman (C2)

Locations Assistant, Lacock
Theodora Van Der Beek (C2)

Script Executive
Susie Conklin

Script Editor
Elizabeth Kilgarriff (C2)

Script Supervisors
Suzanne McGeachan (C1)
Vicki Howe (C2)

Trainee Script Supervisor
Nicoletta Mani (C1)

Production Co-ordinators
Jenny Brassett
Camilla Curtis (C1)

Assistant Co-ordinator
Jen Hudson

Producer's Assistant
Jon Rowe

Production Accountants
Neil Jones (C1)
Sarah Millar (C2)

Assistant Accountants
Carla Self (C1)
Warren Demer (C2)

Cashier
Paul Mafo (C2)

Production Runner
David Harwood (C2)

PA to Judi Dench
Emma-Louise Burke (C2)

Judi Dench's Stand-in
Penny Ryder

Casting Assistant
Camilla Evans

Camera Operators
Roger Pearce (C1)
Hamish Doyne-Ditmas (C2)

Focus Pullers
Adam Coles
Anthony Hugill (C1)
Charlie England (C2)

Clapper/Loaders
Dean Murray (C1)
Alex Golding (C1)
Craig Porter (C2)
Sam Smithard

Digital Technician
Steve Price (C2)

Key Grips
Ronan Murphy (C1)
Keith Mead (C2)

Grips
Simon Thorpe (C1)
Daniel Rake (C1)

Assistant Grip
Martin Clay (C2)

Camera Trainee
Jonathan Tubb (C2)

Gaffers
Alan Martin (C1)
Mark Clayton (C2)

Best Boy
Terry Montague (C1)
Benny Harper (C2)

Electrical Department
James Nesbitt (C1)
David Taylor (C1)
Rob Walton (C1)
Steve Young (C2)
Enrico Faccio (C2)

Boom Operator
Tony Cook

Sound Assistants
Joanna Andrews (C1)
Thayna McLaughlin (C2)
Sam Pullen (C1)

Supervising Art Director
Charmian Adams

Art Director
Mark Kebby

Set Decorator
Trisha Edwards

Production Buyer
Gina Cromwell

Standby Art Directors
Paddy Paddison (C1)
Laura Conway-Gordon (C2)

Assistant Art Directors
Lucy Spofforth (C1)
Antonia Atha (C2)

Art Department Trainee
Lewis Peake (C2)

Property Master
Mike Power

Chargehand Prop
Tom Pleydell-Pearce (C2)

Standby Props
Andy Forrest (C1)
Mike Rawlings (C1)
Noel Cowell (C1)
Damian Butlin (C2)
Campbell Mitchell (C2)

Dressing Props
Charlie Johnson (C1)
Don Santos (C1)
Monty Wilson (C1)
Kevin Fleet (C2)

Construction Manager
Barry Moll

Standby Carpenters
Andrew Fox (C1)
John Gibson

Standby Riggers
Michael Redmond (C1)
Ian Murray (C2)

Standby Stagehands
Steve Davis (C1)
Paul Roberts (C2)

Supervising Painter
Nick Wood

SCENIC ARTIST
Barty Bailey (C2)

SCENIC PAINTERS
Dean Hawley (C1)
Mark Adams (C2)

PAINTERS
Vivien Ball (C2)
Anthony O'Callaghan (C2)
Mary-Pat Sheahan (C2)
Phil Wheeler (C2)

SUPERVISING CARPENTERS
Steve Deane
Roger Wilkins (C2)

CARPENTERS
Geoff Ball (C1)
Mark Collisson (C1)
Charles Hammett (C1)
John New (C1)
John Symons (C1)
Gareth Wilkins
Joe Willmott
Nicholas Clayton (C2)
Barry Lawrence (C2)
Zane McGill (C2)
Richard Mason (C2)
Brian Montgomery (C2)
Sebastian Palmer (C2)
Christopher Sibley-Hale (C2)

SFX SUPERVISOR
Mark Holt

SFX TECHNICIANS
Jamie Weguelin
Patrick O'Sullivan (C1)
James Davis (C1)
John Boundy (C2)
John Savage (C2)

ARTIFICIAL SNOW
Snow Business

COSTUME SUPERVISORS
Mark Ferguson (C1)
Alison Beard (C2)

ASSISTANT COSTUME DESIGN
Charlotte Law

WORKROOM SUPERVISOR
Stephen Miles

COSTUME ASSISTANTS
Helen Ingham (C1)
David Otzen (C1)
Kirsty Wilkinson (C1)
Rob Brown (C2)
Lucy Donowho (C2)
Sunita Singh (C2)

COSTUME TRAINEES
Emma Devonald (C2)
Jenna McGranaghan (C2)

MAKE-UP/HAIR SUPERVISORS
Julie Kendrick (C1)
Karen Z.M. Turner (C1)
Natalie Reid (C2)

MAKE-UP/HAIR ARTISTS
Adele Firth (C1)
Marc Pilcher (C1)
Talli Pachter (C2)
Karen Teitge (C2)

MAKE-UP TRAINEES
Laura Lilley (C1)
Charlie James (C2)
Jade Clarke (C2)

HORSES/CARRIAGES
Steve Dent

HORSEMASTER
Emma Hepple

VOICE COACH
Majella Hurley

ANIMAL TRAINER
Gill Raddings

STUNT CO-ORDINATOR
Nrinder Dhudwar

STUNTS
Stephen Walsh (C1)
Tony Van Silva
Michael Byrch (C1)
Gary Hoptrough (C2)
Levan Doran (C2)

UNIT MEDIC
Dylan Davies

CHOREOGRAPHY ASSISTANT
Wendy Woodbridge

TUTOR
Zoe Barrows

STAGE SECURITY
Paul Kempton (C1)

FACILITIES
Andy Dixon Facilities

CATERING
J&J International

TRANSPORT CAPTAIN
Darren Lean (C1)
Mark Beeton (C2)

PUBLICITY
Annie Frederick (C1)
Cathie Davey (C2)

PICTURE PUBLICITY
Matt Bannister (C1)
Rob Fuller (C2)

STILLS PHOTOGRAPHERS
Nick Briggs (C1)
Laurence Cendrowicz (C2)

TALENT RIGHTS EXECUTIVE
Thalia Reynolds

HISTORICAL ADVISOR
Jenny Uglow

RESEARCH
Pat Silburn

MEDICAL ADVISOR
Dr Martin Scurr MBBC MRCGP
FRCP

MAGIC CONSULTANT
Paul Kieve

MUSIC PRODUCERS
Paul Wing (C1)
Steve McLaughlin (C2)

EPK DIRECTOR
Sven Arnstein

POST-PRODUCTION SUPERVISOR
Sam Lucas

ASSISTANT EDITORS
Jesse Parker (C1)
Supriya Naidu-James (C2)

TRAINEE ASSISTANT EDITOR
Lucy Donaldson (C2)

SOUND EFFECTS EDITORS
Graham Headicar
Catherine Hodgson
Lee Walpole (C2)

DIALOGUE EDITORS
Andre Schmidt (C1)
Iain Eyre (C2)

COLOURIST
Jet Omoshebi (C1)
Gareth Spensley (C2)

ONLINE EDITOR
Shane Warden (C1)
Justin Eely (C2)

VFX SUPERVISOR
Simon Carr (C2)

VFX PRODUCER
Shanaullah Umerji (C2)

TITLES EDITOR
Dolores McGinley (C1)

DIGITAL EFFECTS
Emily Irvine (C1)

POST-PRODUCTION PAPERWORK
Felicia McDonald (C1)
Liz Hill (C2)

PICTURE POST-PRODUCTION
Pepper (C1)
Molinare (C2)

SOUND POST-PRODUCTION
Boom

EXECUTIVE PRODUCER
FOR WGBH
Rebecca Eaton

EXECUTIVE PRODUCER
Kate Harwood

PRODUCED BY
Sue Birtwistle

Chestermead

BBC/WGBH
in association with
Chestermead

Cranford
© BBC 2007
Return to Cranford
© BBC 2009

NB:(C1) denotes work on
Cranford – Series One;
(C2) denotes work on
Cranford – Series Two;
No mark: denotes work
on both series.

Locations

JENKYNS' HOUSE
Exterior
Lacock, Wiltshire

MISS POLE'S HOUSE
Exterior
Lacock

TOMKINSONS' HOUSE
Exterior
Lacock

MRS JAMIESON'S HOUSE
Exterior
Lacock
Interior
The Manor, Byfleet, Surrey

MRS FORRESTER'S COTTAGE
Exterior
Two Yews Cottage, Radnage,
Buckinghamshire

CAPTAIN BROWN'S HOUSE
Exterior
Lacock

MISS GALINDO'S SHOP
Exterior
Lacock

DR HARRISON'S HOUSE
Exterior
Lacock

JOHNSON'S UNIVERSAL STORES
Exterior
Lacock

CRANFORD TOWN BARN
Lacock

CRANFORD STREETS
Lacock

THE ASSEMBLY ROOMS
Ealing Studios

CRANFORD CHURCH
St Mary's, Radnage, Buckinghamshire

WOODLEY
Dorney Court, Berkshire
Bullocks Farm, West Wycombe,
Buckinghamshire

THE GLEBE
Wasing Place, Aldermaston

THORN COTTAGE
Laundry Cottage, Heckfield, Hampshire

PEGGY'S SPRING
Flash Brook, Quarnford, Buxton

CRANFORD ENVIRONS
Ashridge Estate, Hertfordshire

BLUEBELL WOOD
Winkworth Arboretum,
Godalming, Surrey

HANBURY COURT
West Wycombe Park, Buckinghamshire
Syon Park, Brentford, Middlesex

MR CARTER'S OFFICE
Osterley Park, Isleworth, Middlesex

APPLE BARN AND COWSHED
Bullocks Farm, West Wycombe,
Buckinghamshire

GREGSONS' HOVEL
Exterior
Hambleden Estate, Berkshire

TINDEN END COTTAGES
Old Corners Farm, Quarnford,
Staffordshire

**RAILWAY WORKS
AND LIME PIT**
Pitstone Quarry, Hertfordshire

THE RAILWAY
Foxfield Railway,
Stoke-on-Trent, Staffordshire

(All other interiors shot at Ealing,
Pinewood and Shepperton Studios)

GERRY SCOTT (1944–2007)
Who started the journey of *Cranford* with us, and whose talent, friendship and
radiant personality are much missed by all who were fortunate to know her. (*Left*)

ALISON ELLIOTT (1962–2009)
Hair and Make-up Designer on the first series, whose warmth, attention to detail
and kindness inspired us all. (*Right*)

Author Biographies

Sue Birtwistle

Sue started work as an actress with the Belgrade Theatre in Education Company in Coventry, moving to Edinburgh Lyceum Theatre where she became director of the TIE company. She was founding director of Nottingham Playhouse Roundabout Company before joining Thames Television to produce new plays for young people, with writers Andrew Davies, Ken Campbell, Brian Glover and Adrian Mitchell. Her subsequent television work includes *Pride and Prejudice*, William Boyd's *Dutch Girls*, Christopher Hampton's *Hotel Du Lac*, Trevor Griffiths's *Oi For England*, Tony Harrison's *'v.'* and *Scoop*. She is married to film and theatre director Richard Eyre and lives in London.

Susie Conklin

A penchant for English literature and drama led Susie from the American West to London, where she began her career as a production trainee at the BBC and then script editor on *Middlemarch*. She has collaborated with producer Sue Birtwistle on television adaptations of *Pride and Prejudice*, *Emma*, *Wives and Daughters* and *Armadillo*, as well as two books, including *The Making of Pride and Prejudice*. Having script-edited a wide range of other programmes, such as *Band of Gold*, *The Second Coming* and *State of Play*, Susie is now writing original dramas of her own. Educated at Columbia University, she lives with her husband and daughter in Colorado.

Acknowledgements

As with the programmes, so with this book: there are so many people without whom we could not have done it.

We are grateful to all of those in the cast and crew who took the time to share their memories of making *Cranford*. And to the following for allowing their photographs to be used: Ben Smithard, Richard May, Donal Woods, Jon Rowe, Simon Curtis and Suzy McGeachan.

Our thanks also:

To Jenny Uglow, for her generous encouragement with this book and for being our touchstone in all things Gaskell.

To Jon Rowe, whose skills and swiftness in so many areas were invaluable. As Posy Simmonds once remarked: 'Everyone should have a Jon Rowe in their life.' We were lucky to have him in ours during the writing.

To our editors, Richard Atkinson, Natalie Hunt and Janet Illsley, and designer Will Webb, who not only let us have our own fun writing this book, but also let us share theirs in putting it together.

A personal thank you from Susie to Richard and Lorna for dealing so graciously with her absence over the months that this book was written.

We are fortunate indeed to have special contributions in this book from three extraordinarily talented women: Posy Simmonds, Heidi Thomas and Jenny Uglow, all of whom worked with us on *Cranford*. We are delighted and honoured to share these pages with them.

Sue & Susie
June 2010

The Final Word

Eileen Atkins:
'I think this has been the best atmosphere on set of anything I've ever been in. There are various reasons why, but right at the top you've got Judi Dench. She's a brilliant actress who takes the work seriously, but someone who thinks life is to be enjoyed as well, so that filtered down through the cast and crew and you felt everyone loosen up.'

Elizabeth Gaskell:
'We all love Miss Matty, and I somehow think we are all of us better when she is near us.'

First published in 2010

Bloomsbury Publishing Plc, 36 Soho Square, London W1D 3QY
Bloomsbury USA, 175 Fifth Avenue, New York, NY 10010
Bloomsbury Publishing, London, New York, Berlin and Sydney

A CIP catalogue record for this book is available from the British Library.
Cataloging-in-Publication Data is available from the Library of Congress.

UK ISBN 978 1 4088 0938 9
US ISBN 978 1 60819 305 9
10 9 8 7 6 5 4 3 2 1

Project Editor: Janet Illsley
Designer: Will Webb, willwebb.co.uk

Printed and bound in Great Britain by Butler Tanner & Dennis Ltd, Frome and London

All papers used by Bloomsbury Publishing are natural, recyclable products made from wood grown in well-managed forests. The manufacturing processes conform to the environmental regulations of the country of origin.

www.bloomsbury.com/cranford
www.bloomsburyusa.com

Picture credits
Endpapers, map and hand lettering © Posy Simmonds. All other images © BBC Photo Library except: p.11 © Carolyn Djanogly; p.13, p.40. p.41, p.102, p.136, p.155, p.159, p.163 (top), p.187 (bottom), p.204 (bottom left), p.213 (bottom) © Suzy McGeachan; p.15 © Mary Evans Picture Library; pp.17–21, p.187 (top) © Bridgeman Art Library; p.50, p.113, p.215 © Ben Smithard; p.94 © National Trust Picture Library; p.112, p.171 © Richard May; pp.148–9 © Steve Ullathorne (Nicholas Le Prevost), Mitch Jenkins (Lisa Dillon), Simon Emmett (Andrew Buchan), Dillon Bryden (Claudie Blakley and Greg Wise), Bee Gilbert (Finty Williams), Sven Arnstein (Barbara Flynn, Michelle Dockery and Lesley Sharp), Sheila Burnett (Imelda Staunton), Lesley Bruce (Deborah Findlay), Jenny Potter (Selina Griffiths), Sheila Burnett (Jim Carter), Chris Baker (Julia Sawalha), Rob Savage (Alistair Petrie), Cleon Manz (Simon Woods), Ian Phillips-McLaren (Joe McFadden), Carole Latimer (Lesley Manville), Peter Simkin (Rory Kinnear), Simon Annand (Emma Fielding), Steve Lawton (Emma Lowndes), Magnus Hastings (Kimberley Nixon), Gary Duvel (Adrian Scarborough), Sarah Dunn (Debra Gillett), Gabriel Pryce (Jonathan Pryce), Claire Newman-Williams (Tom Hiddleston and Matthew McNulty), Ben King (Jodie Whittaker); p.160 © Wellcome Collection; p.166 © The Art Archive / Museum of London; p.167 (top right), p.176, p.199 (top left), p.204 (top and bottom right), p.209 © Jon Rowe; p.177 © Donal Woods; p.208 (bottom right) © Barbara Flynn; p.208 (bottom left) © Simon Curtis